DR. DICK TIBBITS
WITH STEVE HALLIDAY

FORGIVE
TO
LIVE
Devotional

56 SPIRITUAL INSIGHTS
ON FORGIVENESS
THAT COULD SAVE YOUR LIFE!

FLORIDA
HOSPITAL

Since 1908

FORGIVE TO LIVE DEVOTIONAL

Published by Florida Hospital
683 Winyah Drive, Orlando, FL 32803

TO EXTEND *the* HEALING MINISTRY *of* CHRIST

General Editor: Todd Chobotar
Review Board: Greg Ellis, Len Archer, Richard Duerksen
Photography: Spencer Freeman
Cover Design: Russ McIntosh, Brand Navigation, LLC, BrandNavigation.com
Interior Design: Rainbow Graphics
Additional Graphic Art: Bobby Sagmiller, VisibilityCreative.com
Promotion: Stephanie Rick
Project Coordinator: Lillian Boyd

Published in association with the literary agency of Alive Communications, Inc., 7680 Goddard St, Suite 200, Colorado Springs, CO 80920

ISBN-13: 978-0-9719074-8-5
ISBN-10: 0-9719074-8-X

Printed in the United States of America
07 08 09 10 11 T-S 9 8 7 6 5 4 3 2 1

DEDICATION

To my daughter Jaime, who loves the Lord
in her unique and special way.
What a blessing to be forgiven by your child for your
parenting mistakes!

CONTENTS

Acknowledgements		x
Introduction		xi
Insight 1	When Life Was Fair	1
Insight 2	The Blame Game Begins	4
Insight 3	Turn to Him	7
Insight 4	Choose The Third Option	10
Insight 5	It Sure Didn't Hurt	13
Insight 6	A Great Paradox	16
Insight 7	Justice Is Coming	19
Insight 8	How Many Times?	22
Insight 9	The Only Way to Live	25
Insight 10	How to Love a Lot	28
Insight 11	The "Final Form" of Love	31
Insight 12	A Gift You Can Keep Giving	34
Insight 13	Looking For a Scapegoat	37
Insight 14	The Planks and Sawdust of Sin	40
Insight 15	Who We Are, Not Merely What We Do	43
Insight 16	The Prodigal's Path of Forgiveness	46
Insight 17	No Stone Throwing Here	49
Insight 18	Choosing To Forgive	52
Insight 19	Just This Once	55
Insight 20	Count On It	58
Insight 21	The Work Only Forgiveness Can Do	61

Insight 22 A Sign of Strength   64

Insight 23 Doing What Doesn't Come Naturally   67

Insight 24 Keep Your Eyes on God   70

Insight 25 A Mandatory Option   73

Insight 26 Empathy: A Key to Forgiveness   76

Insight 27 A Love That Is Stronger Than Fate   79

Insight 28 Choose A Bigger Frame   82

Insight 29 Peace and Rest – And Forgiveness   85

Insight 30 The Exhilaration of Acceleration   88

Insight 31 Look and Be Saved   91

Insight 32 A Yoke That Brings Rest   94

Insight 33 Peace for The Journey   97

Insight 34 Cultivating Joy   100

Insight 35 Listening for God's Whisper   103

Insight 36 Grateful for the Delay   106

Insight 37 A Sure Route to Many Sins   109

Insight 38 A Heart Attack's Best Friend   112

Insight 39 The Worst Kind of Anger   115

Insight 40 Don't Let It Stay!   118

Insight 41 Bitter or Better?   121

Insight 42 Forgiveness and the Golden Rule   124

Insight 43 Hope with a Capital H   127

Insight 44	Healing Faith	130
Insight 45	Think of God, Not the Grudge	133
Insight 46	Change the Channel	136
Insight 47	The Health Benefits of Love	139
Insight 48	God's Prescription for Health	142
Insight 49	A Tremendous Source of Strength and Health	145
Insight 50	An Unbreakable Link	148
Insight 51	Don't Try It Yourself	151
Insight 52	A Life Without Poison	154
Insight 53	A Taste of Heaven	157
Insight 54	No Second Thoughts	160
Insight 55	An Eternal Difference	163
Insight 56	Why Did Jesus Come	166
About the Author		169
About Florida Hospital		170

ACKNOWLEDGEMENTS

We all try to do our best. Most of the time we do the right thing - occasionally we fail. When it comes to our children we try extra hard to be perfect parents. I learned a lot about forgiveness raising my daughter. For example, my way is not always the best way...even if father thinks he knows best. So to my daughter, Jaime, who survived my best attempts to perfectly parent her, I dedicate this devotional book. And for her love, patience and encouragement throughout the writing process I want to thank my wife Arta.

I want to acknowledge a few people who made this book possible. Todd Chobotar for his vision for publishing, Stephanie Rick for her marketing ideas, Lillian Boyd for her organization and attention to details, and to Des Cummings for his commitment to see publishing take root at Florida Hospital.

In addition, I want to thank Lars Houmann, Brian Paradis and Don Jernigan for their vision and commitment to promoting Whole Person Health. For his enthusiasm and unwavering support I want to thank my agent Lee Hough and for his wonderful ideas and exceptional wordsmithing I want to thank Steve Halliday.

Finally, I am excited to share with you the reader, the scriptural foundations for the principles of forgiveness found in my book Forgive to Live. May God's words on forgiveness bless your life as it has blessed mine.

INTRODUCTION

Blessed are they whose transgressions are forgiven,
whose sins are covered.

Romans 4:7

Where would we be without forgiveness?

Well, I know of a lot of places we *wouldn't* be without it. For one, without God's forgiveness through Jesus Christ, we'd never be in heaven. For another, we'd never be able to escape the pain of past hurts. Also, relationships would stagnate, if not die, because there would be no way for wounds to heal. And, finally, we would be without hope for the future.

Clearly, forgiveness is a gift that blesses us in many ways. First and foremost, forgiveness makes possible a loving, growing, dynamic relationship with God. It also provides a way of escape from the entrapment of our past. It allows for the possibility of repairing fractured connections to people. And it can bless us with peace for today and hope for tomorrow. In other words, God blesses us with His heavenly forgiveness; others bless us with their earthly forgiveness; and we bless ourselves by choosing to forgive those who have hurt us.

In the daily devotionals that follow, I want to celebrate these many blessings of forgiveness. I want to rejoice in God's forgiveness, exult in the forgiveness others extend to us, and delight in the benefits we receive when we make the choice to forgive. I also want to help you better understand how forgiveness heals physical, mental, and spiritual wounds. And, as best I can, I want to help you see forgiveness in a fresh, challenging, and encouraging way.

I believe my background uniquely qualifies me to address the many benefits of forgiveness. As a licensed mental-health counselor, as a health educator who has studied the mind/body/spirit connection, and as an ordained minister, I have the advantage of seeing the world through three different sets of lenses.

As a counselor, I am trained to see beyond immediate problems to their root causes. Through the use of diagnostic tools and because of my experience with countless others who have dealt with similar difficulties, I can often help bring insight and understanding of what lies behind the problematic symptoms. I can also help people look beyond their resistance to forgiving the one who hurt them in order to see the benefits of forgiveness.

Second, as a trained educator in mind/body/spirit medicine who has more than twenty years of hospital-based healthcare experience, I have observed and studied the many advantages of integrating the best of technology with the best of the human spirit. As I discovered in my research, the practice of forgiveness can lead to improved physical health.

Finally, as an ordained minister, I have yet another resource to guide me—and to help me guide others—through the often bewildering and complex work of living: the Bible. In its inspired pages we find the experiences of men and women of God who face experiences similar to what you and I must deal with on a daily basis. And in their struggle for answers, God provides direction. From their stories we learn a great deal about how to live—especially when life goes wrong. The Bible, more than any other book, is a believer's source of inspiration and healing instruction. Thus, the Bible serves as a guide for everything

I write. In my book *Forgive to Live*, I do not reference specific Scripture passages, as I do not want to create a barrier for any reader who may not accept the Bible as God's inspired truth. But in this devotional I am able to share with you the scriptural principles that underlie and support the concepts of forgiveness I teach in my book.

I have written this devotional from the three perspectives of counseling, medicine, and faith—to help enrich both your understanding and your practice of forgiveness. Furthermore, while all religions teach us that we need to forgive, few have outlined exactly how to do so. To address this gap, in my book *Forgive to Live*, I take a practical, how-to approach to forgiveness and boil down the complex concept of forgiveness into bite-size insights and specific actionable steps.

But forgiveness is more than a behavior to be practiced or a thought process to be learned. It is a spiritual principle to be lived. Therefore, forgiveness is best defined by the One who makes forgiveness possible. So, in this devotional, I will go right to the Word of God to discover our Creator's take on forgiveness. From Him alone will we get the truest, most comprehensive picture of forgiveness possible, for all forgiveness ultimately comes from the Lord. It was Christ's death on the cross that made forgiveness possible in the first place.

I wrote this devotional as a companion volume to the *Forgive to Live* book and workbook. The arrangement of the devotions corresponds to the order of material found in the workbook. So, if you are participating in an eight-week forgiveness-training program, you can read a devotional a day for the entire duration of the program. Doing so will allow you to integrate the Word of God with the practical guidelines offered in the workbook.

This devotional also adds spiritual depth to the *Forgive to Live* book. Reading one devotional each day as you work through the book will help cement your growing understanding of forgiveness. Although the devotionals will not line up perfectly with the order of the topics as they appear in the book, the insights you gain as you study, meditate, and pray will nevertheless enrich and facilitate your forgiveness journey.

Finally, you can also use this devotional on its own as part of your daily quiet time. Its many helpful insights and practical suggestions will enhance your spiritual journey.

However you choose to use these devotional readings, I urge you to keep in mind what a tremendous blessing forgiveness truly is. It really is a gift worth celebrating and pursuing! May you be richly blessed as you drink deeply of the life-giving waters of forgiveness.

INSIGHT 1

WHEN LIFE WAS FAIR

༚༄༅

God saw all that he had made, and it was very good.

Genesis 1:31

Imagine walking through the Garden of Eden before Adam and Eve ate of the forbidden fruit. Everywhere you look, you see beauty, abundance, peace, and harmony. Delight fills your soul as you experience a world without pain, hardship, disease, suffering, or anything else that would make it less than the paradise it truly is.

A goodness fills the air that makes everything seem delicious. Colors seem more vibrant, aromas more delectable, sounds more melodious. And, perhaps best of all, life here is perfectly fair.

Each flower gets exactly the right amount of water and sunshine that it needs to thrive. Each bird soaring in the air above and every beast crawling on the ground below receive precisely whatever they require to grow and prosper. No creature treats another unfairly, and every living thing seems to shout, "This is how life is meant to be!"

And why wouldn't Eden be this way? All this beauty and harmony and fairness was created by a beautiful, kind, and absolutely fair and loving God.

As you wonder at this idyllic scene, you find yourself

rejoicing in the staggering divine wisdom that made it possible. You realize that God, in His perfect wisdom, created all the goodness that is Eden—and you remember that wisdom always does "what is right and just and fair" (Proverbs 1:3). In fact, you recall that God wants to give His wisdom to you and me so that we "will understand what is right and just and fair—every good path" (Proverbs 2:9).

And you certainly see a lot of "good paths" in this unsullied garden! One of them catches your eye, and you decide to do some exploring. As you follow the path through a maze of exotic plants, you enjoy the cool, soft grass beneath your bare feet. After a short walk, you emerge from under a canopy of lush vegetation and step into a gorgeous meadow bursting with sunflowers, poppies, sweet peas, and an amazing assortment of magnificent flowers, the likes of which you've never seen. In the middle of the meadow, several hundred yards away, you spot them— Adam and Eve themselves, hand in hand, laughing and talking and savoring each other's company.

Even from a distance you see the mutual respect, admiration, deep pleasure, and genuine love that each has for the other. Adam gently and tenderly wraps his arms around his beloved wife, and Eve responds to his soft touch with an abandonment that knows no fear or self-consciousness.

And suddenly you find yourself thinking what the other creatures of Eden seemed to be saying just a few minutes before: "This is how life is meant to be!"

You can't visit Eden, but your sense that life should be fair has its roots in that garden. And this sense that life should be fair is in our genes, causing us to yearn for the perfect conditions that once existed in the good world God created.

Of course, the fairness—or, actually, unfairness—of life post-Eden is another matter entirely, and we'll learn how to deal with that soon enough. Now, however, you can rejoice in your saving and sustaining relationship with a good God whose wisdom leads Him—and instructs everyone He created—to do "what is right and just and fair." And that really is how He designed life to be.

TAKE TIME TO PONDER

1. What aspects of your life seem fair to you? Explain.
2. What can you do to help make life fair—or fairer—for others?

TAKE TIME TO PRAY

Father, I praise You for Your good and fair nature. I thank You that I can completely trust You, knowing that You will always do what is right and just and fair. You know, Lord, that sometimes I question why You allow certain things to happen to me. In those moments please remind me of Your faithfulness, help me see evidence of Your love, and enable me to trust in Your grace. After all, You have always been, are now, and forever will be a good and holy and perfect God. I pray in Jesus' name, amen.

THE BLAME GAME BEGINS

And the man said, The woman whom thou gavest to be with me, she gave me of the tree, and I did eat. And the LORD God said unto the woman, What is this that thou hast done? And the woman said, The serpent beguiled me, and I did eat.

Genesis 3:12–13 KJV

Life was free of conflicts, worries, and pain, and Eden was the perfect paradise—exactly what God created it to be.

But then Satan intervened.

It seems the serpent had overheard a conversation between God and Adam. "You are free to eat from any tree in the garden," God had said, "but you must not eat from the tree of the knowledge of good and evil, for when you eat of it you will surely die" (Genesis 2:16–17). Adam and his wife were free to feast on any of the fruits of the garden—except one.

Now, many of us wonder why God would include this potential for disaster in His glorious and perfect garden. Why have such a tree in Eden at all? Some theorize that God did so in order to give Adam and Eve a genuine choice about whether or not they would follow Him willingly and wholeheartedly.

And choose they did. Unfortunately, they made the wrong choice. Satan used God's single prohibition—an instruction designed, as all of His instructions are, for the well-being of His people—to suggest that God is not good and generous, but instead stingy, insecure, capricious, and even untrustworthy.

Once the serpent got Eve alone, he led her to believe that, by withholding the goodies of that tree, God was not being fair in His dealings with her and her husband. In fact, the serpent suggested, God wanted only to keep them utterly subservient and controlled. Could God be any more unfair than that?

Sadly, Eve listened to the wrong voice. And the more she listened, the more unfair God's arrangements seemed. She nodded in agreement as Satan slyly suggested that God's plans were not in her best interest. And soon Eve began to wonder: *How could God really care about me if He intentionally keeps me from the best life has to offer? And He's threatening us with death when we've seen no evidence that such a thing even exists? How unfair! How miserably, horribly, frustratingly unfair!*

So, trusting the Liar and doubting God, Eve ate of the forbidden tree, gave some of its fruit to her husband, and too late discovered that she had been deceived. Now what?

Blame, of course. Even today blame is an extremely popular way for us human beings to deal with our problems. When God confronted Adam and Eve about their disobedience, this blame game began. Adam blamed Eve and even God. Eve blamed the serpent. And surely the serpent would have blamed someone else had he not almost immediately found himself gagging on a mouthful of dust (Genesis 3:14).

Now life in Eden was one sorry mess . . . and life on planet Earth hasn't been the same since. All the heartaches of our brutish history flow from the poison of sinful disobedience and mistrust of God that Adam and Eve introduced to the world that awful day.

Does your heart long for life to be fair? There's nothing wrong with that. The feeling is inborn, an instinctive cry for what was—and what will one day be again. But the hard fact is that life on this planet is no longer fair. Loved ones lie to us. Robbers steal from us. Diseases kill us. The list goes on and on—and none of it is fair.

So how do you respond to the unfairness of life? Your response to life's unfairness will determine in large measure your happiness or bitterness.

TAKE TIME TO PONDER

1. In what situations do you find yourself insisting that life should be fair?
2. Whom do you blame for the unfair things that have happened in your life? What does such blame accomplish?

TAKE TIME TO PRAY

Father, it's hard to live in an unfair world, especially when I know You created it free of sin and therefore a place of fairness and justice. Show me how to best respond to the unfair things that happen to me, and give me the strength to treat others fairly even when I don't feel like it. In Jesus' name, amen.

INSIGHT 3

TURN TO HIM

꿍

To Adam he said, "Because you listened to your wife and ate
from the tree about which I commanded you, 'You must not eat of it,'
cursed is the ground because of you;
through painful toil you will eat of it all the days of your life."

Genesis 3:17

With one bite or maybe two, the whole world changed. In an instant Adam and Eve were transported from paradise to a much harsher reality.

In the pristine garden, they had simply picked fruit whenever they felt hungry, and the fresh delicacies were always extraordinarily delicious. God put everything Adam and Eve needed within their reach for their nourishment and enjoyment.

But all that changed the moment they bit into the one fruit God had placed off limits. It wasn't long before Adam saw weeds sprout up among his crops in an attempt to choke out the food he needed to sustain both himself and his family. So Adam discovered the grueling work of tilling, planting, weeding, and harvesting, and he soon learned how unfair farming and the capricious weather could be. Some years he enjoyed a bountiful harvest, and other years a meager one despite putting in the same amount of effort. And so the evening meal—once a greatly anticipated gift, a time of pure enjoyment—became the less-than-reliable result of his backbreaking work.

And life was no easier for Eve. Can you imagine her first pregnancy? She had no mother to talk her through those forty weeks and no girlfriend to compare notes with. At first Eve probably found it exciting to notice a new life fluttering and then kicking within her, but those contractions were a rude surprise when the time came to deliver her first son!

And her pain did not end with her excruciating childbirth experiences. Yes, Eve went through the whole process again with her second son, and who knows how many children after that? She might have come to understand the process, but every time she gave birth, the pain was every bit as raw and intense as the first time. Probably even worse than this physical pain, though, was the emotional pain from her fractured relationship with her husband. After God had said, "Your desire will be for your husband, and he will rule over you" (Genesis 3:16), the perfectly harmonious relationship they had enjoyed in the garden had vanished forever.

And then, years later, both Adam and Eve had to endure the tragedy of their oldest son murdering his innocent brother. God had warned them that death would surely accompany any decision to eat the fruit He had forbidden—and now, in the cold, lifeless body of their second born, they saw the substance of God's warning played out in their lives. Their loss and heartache must have seemed more than they could bear. How much pain and sorrow could two people endure?

Imagine how Adam and Eve must have longed for the old days in Eden, the time before they disobeyed and the Lord sent them out of their earthly paradise. Was it fair for God to heap all this suffering and misery upon them?

They'd only eaten one piece of forbidden fruit. Didn't this punishment far outweigh the crime?

We don't know if Adam and Eve ever asked such questions, but we do know that, after some time, they no longer blamed God for what had happened. At one point they apparently acknowledged their fault, repented of their prideful disobedience, and turned to God for forgiveness. That process seems to lie behind Eve's humble words after she gave birth to Seth: "God has granted me another child in place of Abel, since Cain killed him" (Genesis 4:25). Gone is her anger and bitterness.

When you face overwhelming difficulties, do you blame God? Do you complain about His negligence, His lack of care, or His seeming unwillingness to grant you relief from your troubles? Or do you admit the truth about your guilt—as Adam and Eve apparently did—and turn to Him for mercy, grace, and forgiveness?

TAKE TIME TO PONDER

1. For what difficulty or tragedy in your life, if any, are you blaming God?
2. What role might you have played in bringing about some of the trouble you face?

TAKE TIME TO PRAY

Father, it's not easy to live in a broken world. Too often I find myself wanting to blame others for my troubles— and sometimes I even want to blame You. Please forgive me for my hard heart and help me turn to You in trust and faith. Help me lean more on You each day. In Jesus' name, amen.

INSIGHT 4

CHOOSE THE THIRD OPTION

Bear with each other and forgive whatever grievances
you may have against one another.

Colossians 3:13

When life is not fair, what can you do? Most of the time, you have three options:

1. You can whine to the people around you, who can do nothing to change the problem.
2. You can appeal to the person who harmed you to make things right.
3. You can quit being a victim and instead work on finding a solution that will keep you moving ahead in life.

If we're honest, most of us would have to admit that we tend to opt for the whining. For one thing, that option is the easiest of the three. We don't have to confront the person who hurt us, we don't have to take responsibility for the part we may have played in the incident, and we don't have to consider what we need to do to get our lives back on track. All we have to do is open our mouths and complain—and, as illogical as it is, we imagine that, by complaining to others, we're restoring a little of the balance that the unfair incident took away. In other words—and still illogically—we think we're making the other person "pay" for what he or she did to us. And by doing so we hope to start balancing the scales of justice.

Of course, our complaining does nothing to restore any sense or degree of balance. Furthermore, while we think we're making a strong case for ourselves, it's not long before the people we complain to want to run away from our constant whining about how unfair life is.

Now to the second option. It makes perfect sense to go to the person who harmed you and seek an apology or even restitution. But far too often that person simply refuses to do either. So what do you do now? Sometimes it is both legitimate and useful to appeal to someone in authority—to a judge, for example, or a police officer—in order to rectify an unjust situation. That's part of what the law exists to do. Usually, however, the "crime" against you simply doesn't warrant such an action. Would you really ask a judge to force your mother-in-law to apologize for her unkind comment? Would you approach the local sheriff to jail a co-worker for lying about you? Probably not. So what option do you have?

You can move on with your life. You can choose to forgive.

Now let me explain how this truth relates to you. When someone hurts you, you probably see that person as the strong one, the one with all the power. So you try to obtain an apology, to get the person to admit the wrong. After all, that would weaken the individual's apparent invincibility, wouldn't it? But until that happens, you feel powerless to do anything, and you remain helpless.

Forgiveness, however, changes your sense of weakness and helplessness. When you choose to forgive, *you* become the strong one. You free yourself to move on from the hurt, which means the person who hurt you no longer has the ability to keep you stuck. By forgiving that person, you are no longer at the whim or mercy of someone else.

I like what my friend—and forgiveness expert—Fred Luskin says about the choice to forgive. He insists that when you choose to forgive, you "become a hero instead of a victim in the story you tell. Forgiveness means that even though you are wounded, you choose to hurt and suffer less. Forgiveness means you become a part of a solution."

This very day, will you choose forgiveness and, with it, the power to move on with life? Or will you continue to whine about the person who hurt you, thereby remaining powerless and stuck exactly where you don't want to be? Will you continue to be a victim, letting the bully throw sand in your face, or will you exercise some of your strength and forgive the one who hurt you?

TAKE TIME TO PONDER

1. What are you doing to try to get someone to make up for an injustice done to you?
2. If you have not yet considered forgiveness, why not?

TAKE TIME TO PRAY

Father, I don't like the feelings of powerlessness and helplessness that have plagued me in this situation. I don't want to remain trapped in a hurtful past. I don't want to be a complainer, so please help me choose to make the healing choice to forgive. In Jesus' name, amen.

INSIGHT 5

IT SURE DIDN'T HURT

⫷

While they were stoning him, Stephen prayed, "Lord Jesus, receive my
spirit." Then he fell on his knees and cried out, "Lord, do not hold this
sin against them." When he had said this, he fell asleep.

Acts 7:59–60

Have you ever been attacked for telling the truth? Maybe
someone asked for your honest opinion, but when you
gave it as graciously as you could, you were blasted. Or
perhaps you brought up a fact that others did not want to
hear and you were made to feel as though your point of
view was the problem.

How do you tend to respond to such hostile outbursts?
Do you get angry? Do you try to shrug off the incident or
withdraw from the conversation? Or do you exercise the
power of forgiveness?

"But they don't deserve to be forgiven!" you say. "Why
should I extend to them the courtesy of forgiveness when
they didn't extend to me any courtesy at all?"

Well, you might want to ask the apostle Stephen that
question.

The book of Acts calls Stephen "a man full of faith and
of the Holy Spirit" (Acts 6:5). Through this man who was
"full of God's grace and power," God "did great wonders

and miraculous signs among the people" (6:8). So, with credentials like that, why did Stephen end up under a pile of stones? Because he told the truth. People didn't want to hear that truth, so they stoned Stephen to death. (And you think *you* are being persecuted!)

Stephen did not return hatred for hatred despite the crowd's unfair treatment of him. No one in the bloodthirsty crowd ever admitted any wrongdoing, apologized to Stephen for hating the messenger as well as the message, or asked him to forgive their intolerance. So what did the apostle do?

Stephen forgave his killers. "Lord," he cried out just before he died, "do not hold this sin against them" (Acts 7:60). Since Stephen had chosen to live a life of forgiveness, he was prepared to offer forgiveness even in his most terrifying hour. And in doing so, he followed the example of his Lord Jesus, who had prayed for those who crucified Him: "Father, forgive them, for they do not know what they are doing" (Luke 23:34).

Is such a response natural? Of course not. Is it easy? Hardly. Left to ourselves, we don't want to forgive those who hurt us; we want to get back at them so they will experience the kind of pain they have caused us. The only effective way to consistently overcome these, our worst impulses, is to make sure that we, like Stephen, are full of faith, grace, divine power, and the Holy Spirit. And those traits come with being in relationship with Jesus and trusting Him with your life.

By forgiving those who attacked him, Stephen apparently didn't change anyone's mind. Stephen didn't have the ability to change what anyone else did, but he could control how he responded to those actions. And, by using his last breath to forgive rather than curse the men who were opposing him, Stephen knew peace in his soul.

Likewise, you can't control what other people do, but you can *always* control how you respond. They might hold a grudge, but you don't have to. They might remain angry, but you can let go of anger by forgiving. And that forgiveness changes and benefits you: it keeps you from becoming bitter, focused on your pain, and stuck in the hurt of the past.

And you never know the impact your extension of forgiveness might have on someone else. Consider that an angry young man named Saul watched Stephen die that day—and not too long afterward he also put his faith in Christ. Today we know Saul as the apostle Paul. Did Stephen's prayer for forgiveness help bring Saul to Christ? There can be no doubt that millions through the ages have been blessed by the writings of Paul because Stephen was a forgiving person.

TAKE TIME TO PONDER

1. When you feel persecuted or misunderstood, what possible courses of action can you choose from?
2. Had you been Stephen, do you think you would have responded with forgiveness? Why or why not? Explain.

TAKE TIME TO PRAY

Father, I need Your help if I am to truly forgive people who hurt me. Please grow in me a forgiving heart like Stephen's, so that when someone wrongs me, Your Spirit within me will enable me to do what I might not want to do on my own. In Jesus' name, amen.

INSIGHT 6

A GREAT PARADOX

Do not seek revenge or bear a grudge against one of your people,
but love your neighbor as yourself. I am the LORD.

Leviticus 19:18

Revenge.

When someone does something to harm us, we often entertain thoughts of revenge. *If I could just get back at her and make her pay for what she did*, we may think, *then life would be fair*.

Years ago when a company I had poured my life into gave me the infamous pink slip, I almost immediately started fantasizing about what I could do to get back at those people responsible for my layoff. I never followed through on my fantasy, but I couldn't let go of the thought of getting back at them in some way.

Of course, thoughts like these are nothing new. The Bible tells an ancient story of hoped-for vengeance in the book of Judges. An evil man named Abimelech murdered seventy half-brothers in order to rule Shechem. Only his brother Jotham escaped. When Jotham heard that the people of Shechem were about to anoint Abimelech their king, he climbed a neighboring peak and shouted: "Now if you have acted honorably and in good faith when you made

Abimelech king, and if you have been fair to [my father] and his family . . . may Abimelech be your joy, and may you be his, too! But if you have not, let fire come out from Abimelech and consume you, citizens of Shechem and Beth Millo, and let fire come out from you, citizens of Shechem and Beth Millo, and consume Abimelech!" (Judges 9:16, 19–20).

Then, fearing for his life, Jotham ran away. You can clearly feel compassion for Jotham in his pain and anger. Who would not feel the way he felt? The truth was hard to face: Jotham could do nothing to change the situation, and, clearly, he was never going to get an apology.

So how would Jotham choose to live the rest of his life? Would he remain trapped in his own fantasies of revenge, or would he forgive and move on with his life? Those aren't easy questions to answer.

What would you do if you were in circumstances similar to Jotham's? What fantasies of revenge lurk in the corners of your mind regarding any painful and unfair experiences from the past? Who has hurt you so deeply that vengeance is the only way you can imagine evening the score? And are you replaying your plan of revenge over and over in your mind?

There's just one problem with this strategy: revenge doesn't work. The truth is that you never win when you try to use revenge to even the score.

An eye for an eye and a tooth for a tooth may seem like ideal justice, but it's not. "You have heard that it was said, 'Eye for eye, and tooth for tooth,'" Jesus declared, "But I tell you, Do not resist an evil person. If someone strikes you on the right cheek, turn to him the other also" (Matthew 5:38–39). If we ignore Jesus' instruction, we can expect pretty ugly results. As Mahatma Gandhi once remarked, "If we practice an eye for an eye and a tooth for a tooth, soon the whole world will be blind and toothless."

Furthermore, fantasies of revenge keep you locked in your painful past. When you keep hitting the rewind button and listen over and over again to the angry story playing in your head, you're allowing the person who hurt you to keep on hurting you. You're actually putting yourself deeper in the hole.

God supplies only one antidote for the human desire for revenge and the natural tendency to hold on to grudges—forgiveness. Only by forgiving the person who hurt you can you let go of your anger and know peace in your soul.

And, yes, there is a great paradox here. Vengeance seems fair, but it gets you nothing but more pain. And forgiveness seems unfair, but it enables you to move on with your life and pursue the things that bring you joy. So the issue of forgiveness boils down to this question: do you want more pain or more joy?

Take Time to Ponder

1. What fantasies do you have about getting even with someone who has harmed you?
2. What impact have these fantasies had on your life? What better option could you choose—and what's keeping you from doing so?

Take Time to Pray

Father, I know You have said in Your Word, "It is mine to avenge; I will repay." Yet I can't seem to stop thinking about what this person did to me and how I could get even. Please change my heart and teach me how to forgive, so I can go on with my life. In Jesus' name, amen.

INSIGHT 7

JUSTICE IS COMING

And will not God bring about justice for his chosen ones, who cry out to him day and night? Will he keep putting them off? I tell you, he will see that they get justice, and quickly.

Luke 18:7–8

Forgiveness is hard work. It doesn't come naturally to any of us. Many of us, however, find it easier to forgive when we remind ourselves that God will carry out complete justice one day—and that's tough to remember because, as we look around today, His justice can be hard to find.

Jesus spoke about this eventual justice when He declared, "There is nothing concealed that will not be disclosed, or hidden that will not be made known" (Matthew 10:26). And the apostle Paul informed us, "The sins of some men are obvious, reaching the place of judgment ahead of them; the sins of others trail behind them" (1 Timothy 5:24). We can be confident that no one ultimately gets away with anything. We don't have to worry that God will ever give up His commitment to fairness. After all, His holy and just nature will never change.

Why, then, does God sometimes seem to let unfairness rule the day? When something painfully unfair happens to us, why doesn't He act immediately to make things right?

Jesus got to the heart of this issue in the somewhat odd parable of the unjust judge. Over the years this parable has confused and even alarmed some believers.

In this story Jesus described a judge "who neither feared God nor cared about men" (Luke 18:2). One day, seeking justice against some unnamed persecutor, a destitute widow came to see him. The judge coldly ignored her request to present her case. Day after day the widow returned to ask him for help, and day after day the judge refused. But the widow did not give up, and finally the judge relented—not out of concern for the woman or respect for God, but because he wanted to rid himself of a pest.

This is where the parable concerns some people. They wonder, *Is Jesus telling me that God is somehow like this unjust judge? That He doesn't care enough about me to deal with my problems? That the only way I can get Him to act on my behalf is by pestering Him to death?*

Happily for all of us, that's not the point of the story at all. To the contrary, Jesus was contrasting the judge's grumpiness with the love of God. If a cruel judge will actually serve justice if we persist in our request, how much more will our loving God bring justice to us? So, while it may *seem* as if God is putting us off, it's not because He doesn't care about us. In fact, He will make *all* things right and just as quickly as possible (Luke 18:8). God will not delay in administering justice one second longer than is absolutely necessary.

And it's actually a very good thing that God doesn't lower His hammer of justice the moment an injustice occurs. If He did, where would that leave you and me? After all, we're not only the recipients of injustice; sometimes we're its perpetrators. So we would be wise to remember the apostle Paul's warning: "Each of us will give an account of himself to God" (Romans 14:12). We might not feel so eager for God to instantaneously mete out His perfect justice on those who hurt us if we considered how often we deserve that same fearful response to our own acts of injustice.

Still, it does help to remember that God is utterly and totally committed to what is right. Again, it may seem to us that He's delaying His justice far too long, but the apostle Peter reminded us, "The Lord is not slow in keeping his promise, as some understand slowness. He is patient with you, not wanting anyone to perish, but everyone to come to repentance" (2 Peter 3:9). God delights in forgiveness— and that's good news for all of us.

TAKE TIME TO PONDER

1. Do you expect God to be kind to you? How do you feel about His being kind to people who hurt you?
2. Respond to this statement: "No sin goes unpunished; either Jesus pays for the believer's sin, or the unbeliever pays for his or her own sin." Why would embracing this truth help you forgive those who hurt you?

TAKE TIME TO PRAY

Father, thank You for being so amazingly patient with me. Thank You for forgiving me when I placed my faith in Christ. I praise You for being so completely holy and righteous and fair—and for assuring me that You will one day set all things right. In Jesus' name, amen.

INSIGHT 8

HOW MANY TIMES?!

꣞

*Then Peter came to Jesus and asked, "Lord, how many times
shall I forgive my brother when he sins against me? Up to seven
times?" Jesus answered, "I tell you, not seven times,
but seventy-seven times."*

Matthew 18:21–22

Some people just have a knack for getting things wrong.
Have you ever met someone like this? Maybe he spills cof-
fee on your desk at work every time he passes by: "Oh,
man, Bob. I'm so sorry. Do you have a napkin handy?" Or
perhaps she has a way of handing out "compliments" that
really sting. It helps only a little that she offers a hasty apology as soon as she sees your face fall and realizes what she
said.

Generally, these folks don't mean any harm; they're just
social bumblers. These *faux pas* come naturally to them.
They feel genuinely sorry for the damage they cause, but
they never quite figure out how to stop breaking things in
the first place.

Do you have anyone like this in your life? Someone who
keeps doing the same wrong thing over and over again? If
you do, you may have found yourself asking Peter's question: "Just how many times do I have to forgive that person?"

The Pharisees of Jesus' day had a rule for almost every situation imaginable. On the matter of forgiveness, for instance, they very magnanimously decreed that if you forgave someone for the same thing on seven different occasions, then you had exceeded the requirements and could consider yourself duly righteous—and if the jerk messed up an eighth time, you could let 'em have it!

Peter knew about this line of legal reasoning, so when he asked Jesus his question, he probably thought he'd be commended for being so generous. After all, how many times could a mere mortal be expected to forgive the same person for doing the same rotten thing over and over again?

As Peter stood there, smiling and certain he was about to receive a gold star, a bracing gust of divine reality from the Master suddenly blew away his smug little grin. Essentially, Jesus told Peter that while forgiving someone seven times was nice, God asks His children to stop counting altogether. In other words, believers are to forgive as God has forgiven them—and the prophet Micah told us that He hurls *all* our sins "into the depths of the sea" (Micah 7:19).

Jesus' answer created a problem not only for Peter, but for all of us. You see, I may need to forgive someone over and over again for many mistakes and bad choices. But I may also need to forgive those mistakes and bad choices over and over again in my mind every time my old feelings of resentment surface.

When those feelings do resurface, does it mean I haven't truly forgiven? I don't think so.

Very few of us entirely forgive a hurt the first time we offer forgiveness—or, for that matter, the second or sometimes even the fiftieth time. Thoughts of hurt and/or retaliation may never vanish entirely (although in some circumstances they do). But just because your forgiveness isn't finished doesn't mean it's not genuine. You may need to mentally forgive this person hundreds of times.

Think of forgiveness as something like the process of healing an open wound. Just because healing doesn't take place all at once doesn't mean it isn't happening at all. The very presence of a scab means that the body is in the process of repairing itself. It simply takes time to finish.

In a similar way, if you need to forgive someone seven times (or seventy-seven times) for the same thing, keep at it. You'll get there eventually. Ultimately, the real question is not "How many times have I forgiven this person?" Rather, it's "Do I—who have been forgiven totally and repeatedly by God—dare withhold my forgiveness from another person even once?"

TAKE TIME TO PONDER

1. Who in your life—if anyone—are you still in the process of forgiving "seventy-seven" times? Explain.
2. Does forgiveness mean allowing someone to repeatedly do the same terrible thing, or can forgiveness include setting up firm boundaries to protect oneself? Explain.

TAKE TIME TO PRAY

Father, help me stop counting the number of times I forgive someone for the same offense. Teach me to cast those hurtful acts and words into the depths of the sea, as You do with my offenses. And remind me that even if my forgiveness isn't finished, that doesn't mean it's not genuine. In Jesus' name, amen.

THE ONLY WAY TO LIVE

*The servant's master took pity on him, canceled
the debt and let him go.*

Matthew 18:27

What's the largest financial debt you've ever forgiven?
Ten dollars? Fifty? A thousand? A million?

What's the most significant moral debt you've ever forgiven? Was it theft? Adultery? Lying? Betrayal? Murder?

These two experiences, taken together, nevertheless fall
infinitely short of the monstrous debts God has forgiven
you and me. We will probably never fully understand the
extent of our wrongdoing, paid for by His Son on the cross.
Therefore, when God asks us to forgive the people who
injure us, He's not speaking from some ivory tower in far-
away heaven. He's speaking as One who has traveled a
rougher road of forgiveness than we could ever imagine. In
that vein, consider Jesus' parable of the unmerciful servant.

A man who served a wealthy king had somehow
amassed a staggering debt of ten thousand talents—untold
millions of dollars in today's currency. To get some perspective on the enormous size of this debt, consider that, at
the time of Jesus, the entire Roman provinces of Judea,
Idumea, and Samaria paid only six hundred talents in taxes

each year. Clearly, this was a gargantuan debt the man had no hope of repaying. Even if he and his family were sold into slavery—an option the king considered—a top-notch slave in those days garnered a price of only one talent, while most slaves brought just one tenth of that amount. Jesus wanted us to understand that the man could *never* repay the debt he owed. Yet when this servant begged for mercy, the king forgave him the entire amount.

And how did the man respond to this extravagant mercy and grace? Incredibly, he immediately went out and found someone who owed him one hundred denarii (most common laborers of that day earned about one denarius a day) and demanded repayment. When the frightened man begged for time to gather the amount he owed, the reprehensible servant had him thrown into prison.

When the king heard about what had happened, he was enraged. He summoned this miserable servant to court, reinstated the man's entire debt, and then "turned him over to the jailers to be tortured, until he should pay back all he owed" (Matthew 18:34). That's tough stuff! And Jesus added an equally tough moral to His story for you and me: "This is how my heavenly Father will treat each of you unless you forgive your brother from your heart" (v. 35).

The whole point of the parable is to show us the shocking incongruity between accepting God's forgiveness for our galaxy-sized debt but refusing to forgive others the flea-sized debts they owe us. Our willingness to forgive those who wrong us is a sign that the Holy Spirit dwells within us, and our failure to forgive suggests that we have not truly accepted God's forgiveness. In fact, I would say that one good way to know that we have come to genuine faith in Jesus is our willingness to forgive those who hurt us. Since the Spirit of God longs to forgive, a stubborn, if not permanent, refusal to forgive may well indicate the absence of God's Spirit in our life. This truth should drive us to our knees and help us recognize the significance of our unwillingness to forgive.

While it may take us some time to sincerely forgive those who hurt us, we must never rule out forgiveness as an option. The Bible commands us to "forgive as the Lord forgave you" (Colossians 3:13) and, in case we miss the point, in another place we are told to "be kind and compassionate to one another, forgiving each other, just as in Christ God forgave you" (Ephesians 4:32).

If you want to reflect the nature of your heavenly Father—and that's one reason why He created you—forgiveness is the only way to live.

TAKE TIME TO PONDER

1. Have you accepted the bountiful forgiveness God offers you? If not, what is keeping you from accepting God's forgiveness for your sins?
2. Why would someone's flat refusal to forgive suggest that he or she has not received the Lord's forgiveness?

TAKE TIME TO PRAY

Father, You know that I sometimes struggle to forgive. But You also know that I want to become more and more like You, and that desire means I need to learn how to forgive even as You have forgiven me. So break down the resistance in my heart and fill me with Your forgiving Spirit. In Jesus' name, amen.

INSIGHT 10

HOW TO LOVE A LOT

But he who has been forgiven little loves little.
Luke 7:47

We live in an age that glorifies self. Who knows when it began, but back in 1966 after the late John Lennon proclaimed the Beatles "more popular than Jesus," it became clear that self-centeredness was the prevailing sentiment of the times.

Whether it's because we've listened too attentively to a zillion skewed messages about loving ourselves or read too many books about building up our self-worth, large numbers of us have come to believe that we're pretty great—and certainly better than most of the world's rabble.

Consider, for instance, the top-rated television program *American Idol*. In the first few shows of every new season, we meet scores of would-be contestants, many of whom have such appalling singing voices that it actually hurts to hear them yowl. Yet when the judges advise them to choose a different career path, many respond with bewilderment, anger, defiance, and often a truckload of bleeped-out expletives. They just *know* they're fabulous, so how could anyone possibly think otherwise? Their critics must be stupid, deaf, envious, ill, jealous, narrow-minded, out-of-touch, silly, ignorant, or just plain mistaken.

Often this same attitude is evident in our opinion of our personal moral character. We, too, tend to think we're really great. Even when we do terrible, outrageous things, we see the behavior as an anomaly, a mere lapse in judgment, a temporary and uncharacteristic expression of who we really are—which is, of course, some pretty wonderful folks.

Sometimes when we have a hard time forgiving someone, the real reason can be traced to our false belief that we haven't been forgiven for all that much—after all, we're pretty good people. Why would anyone need to forgive *us*?

Unfortunately, this faulty attitude has been around a very long time. Way back in Jesus' day, the Pharisees suffered from it. One time, for instance, a Pharisee invited Jesus to a dinner party, and "a woman who had lived a sinful life in that town" crashed the party (Luke 7:37). When she saw Jesus, she wet His feet with her tears and then dried them with her hair, a very public act of repentance and gratitude—and the dinner host silently resented Jesus for allowing such a "sinner" to touch Him (v. 39).

Jesus, of course, knew the man's heart. So He told a short story to make the point that those who recognize how much they have been forgiven respond to the Forgiver with great love. Those of us who are largely blind to our sins, however, see no point in showing Him such extravagant love. Earlier, Jesus had made roughly the same point when He said, "It is not the healthy who need a doctor, but the sick. I have not come to call the righteous, but sinners to repentance" (Luke 5:31–32).

While all of us human beings are sin-sick, not all of us recognize this terminal condition. While all of us need great forgiveness, not all of us think we do. Those of us who admit our illness and confess our great need for forgiveness, however, find ourselves filled with the divine love and power that enable us to offer forgiveness to those who need it from us.

Consider the wisdom of Dr. Martin Luther King Jr.: "We must develop and maintain the capacity to forgive. He who is devoid of the power to forgive is devoid of the power to love. There is some good in the worst of us and some evil in the best of us. When we discover this, we are less prone to hate our enemies."

TAKE TIME TO PONDER

1. In what ways has being forgiven—by God and by people you have hurt—affected your life? Be specific.
2. When you do not feel like forgiving, what can you do to change your attitude?

TAKE TIME TO PRAY

Father, I thank You that You have done everything necessary to bring me into a loving relationship with You. Help me, as a follower of Jesus, to see more clearly how much You have forgiven me. Then, Lord, give me the strength I need to offer forgiveness to others. In Jesus' name, amen.

INSIGHT 11

THE "FINAL FORM" OF LOVE

⳾⸎⳾

And when you stand praying, if you hold anything against anyone,
forgive him, so that your Father in heaven may forgive you your sins.

Mark 11:25

One morning my friend John sat down in a favorite chair at home to pray. He began by praising God for His goodness, confessing a few sins, and thanking Him for some unexpected answers to prayer. Then John started asking for the Lord's divine intervention in a number of areas. As John's prayers rounded the globe on behalf of several missionary friends, the Lord seemed to suddenly yank his attention from important transcontinental concerns to something a lot closer to home: a friend who had snubbed him a few days before. No matter how hard John tried to get back to his original train of thought—surely the more spiritual track, he thought—an image of this friend continued to pop up in his mind.

Greatly annoyed by this "interruption," John stopped praying—until he recalled Jesus' words from the Gospel of Mark: "And when you stand praying, if you hold anything against anyone, forgive him, so that your Father in heaven may forgive you your sins." John knew that this verse was

31

God's message to him, so he decided to obey this command and forgive his friend.

What would happen in our churches, communities, neighborhoods, and homes if we took seriously the Master's simple—but not always easy!—instruction outlined in this verse? Why is it that we tend to consider "religious" activities more important and spiritual than forgiveness, an act Jesus valued so highly? Are we ever more spiritual than when we follow Christ's example and forgive those who have hurt us?

Consider what Reinhold Niebuhr says about the place of forgiveness in our life:

> Nothing worth doing is completed in our lifetime;
>   Therefore, we are saved by hope.
> Nothing true or beautiful or good makes complete sense in any immediate context of history;
>   Therefore, we are saved by faith.
> Nothing we do, however virtuous, can be accomplished alone.
>   Therefore, we are saved by love.
> No virtuous act is quite as virtuous from the standpoint of our friend or foe as from our own;
>   *Therefore, we are saved by the final form of love, which is forgiveness.*

When you forgive, you are more like Jesus than you may be at any other time in your earthly life.

I've also noticed how God tends to remind me of my unfinished business—of forgiveness I've not yet extended—just when I'm having a good time being religious. Sometimes it happens while I'm in church. Other times it happens while I'm at home reading the Bible or enjoying a favorite Christian author. Right when I'm feeling especially holy, the Lord knocks on my heart and seems to say, "Psssst! Hey, Dick! While I appreciate the sentiment here, I'd really rather you deal with that nasty grudge you're holding against [<u>fill in the blank</u>]. If you really want to connect with Me, that's the way to do it. You can always be religious a little later."

Prayer is great. Worship is great. Reading the Bible is great. Listening to a sermon is great. But if we want to connect with God's loving heart, what can compare to following Jesus' example and offering forgiveness to those who have hurt us? That is "the final form" of love.

TAKE TIME TO PONDER

1. What do you believe is the best reason to forgive someone who has hurt or offended you?
2. What would you lose if you forgave a person you're struggling to forgive—and what would you gain?

TAKE TIME TO PRAY

Father, in the Old Testament You tell us that You desire our obedience more than our sacrifices, and in the New Testament You tell us that You value our willingness to extend forgiveness to others over our religious activity. So please help me to increasingly reflect Your heart of love by making forgiveness a top priority in my life. In Jesus' name, amen.

INSIGHT 12

A GIFT YOU CAN KEEP GIVING

꙯

Freely you have received, freely give.
Matthew 10:8

When I was a boy, I got excited every time Christmas rolled around. I loved seeing my name on some of the shiny packages under the tree. Once I identified them, I anxiously awaited the moment I could tear into them and start enjoying the awesome treasures hiding within.

Although I'm a lot older now, I still enjoy Christmas. I still like singing "Jingle Bells." I still enjoy seeing the Christmas tree all aglow and decorated with mementos of Christmas past. And I still glory in the gospel truth about the star of Bethlehem and the long-awaited birth of Jesus the Messiah. Even today I think it's fun to see presents under the tree—but that's where my routine has changed. Oh, I still like to get cool presents, but these days I find a lot more enjoyment in watching other people (especially little people like grandkids) open their gifts. I love to hear their squeals of delight as they receive that "just right" present.

And I suppose this is true for most of us. The more mature we get, the more pleasure we receive from giving. Oh, we still like to receive, but our smiles grow broader and our eyes grow brighter when we see people we love truly enjoy a gift we've chosen just for them.

I'm learning that the gift of forgiveness works the same way. Oh, I definitely like to receive it when I mess up, but I feel even better inside when I can humbly offer that gift to another. That's why, when I hear Jesus' words "freely you have received, freely give," I think of forgiveness. Since I have freely received God's gift of forgiveness, I am able to—and I should—freely give it to others.

Behind this principle of giving to others what we have abundantly received from God is an attitude of gratitude. If we don't feel grateful for what we have received, then we must not feel very blessed by it. And if we aren't feeling blessed by God's gift, then we have not truly received it. If we had, we would feel so overjoyed that we would naturally share it with others. Forgiveness works like a river. If we hold on to the forgiveness we've received rather than letting it flow freely through us, our lack of forgiveness becomes a stagnant pond—ugly, smelly, and more likely to carry disease than health.

Are you feeling blessed by God's gift of forgiveness—or have you not fully and freely received it? Are you letting forgiveness flow through you like the life-giving river it is?

Just before Jesus went to the cross, He celebrated the Last Supper. At one point in that meal, He raised a cup of wine and announced, "This is my blood of the covenant, which is poured out for many for the forgiveness of sins" (Matthew 26:28). Jesus *poured out* His blood generously and freely—He didn't portion it out in a miserly or stingy manner—so that we can experience the wonder and grace of His forgiveness.

The apostle Paul put it like this: "For you know the grace of our Lord Jesus Christ, that though he was rich, yet for your sakes he became poor, so that you through his poverty might become rich" (2 Corinthians 8:9). This wise man of God also taught his friends, "You will be made rich in every way so that you can be generous on every occasion, and through us your generosity will result in thanksgiving to God" (2 Corinthians 9:11).

Paul had material gifts in mind, but this same principle holds true with forgiveness. God makes us rich in forgiveness so we can generously offer forgiveness "on every occasion." And when we do, people can't help but give thanks to God.

Forgiveness is the one gift you and I can keep on giving. In fact, as you continue to receive the Lord's generous gift of forgiveness for your sins, you will find yourself more able to continue giving that gift to others.

TAKE TIME TO PONDER

1. Why do you think it is important to be a forgiving person? Give three or four reasons.
2. In what ways might your decision to forgive others change your life?

TAKE TIME TO PRAY

Father, help me move beyond the struggle to forgive so that I can reach a place where it becomes a real joy. You have freely forgiven me; now enable me to freely give that gift to others—not begrudgingly, but freely; not just because I should, but because I want to, for Your sake. In Jesus' name, amen.

LOOKING FOR A SCAPEGOAT?

*The goat will carry on itself all their sins to a solitary place;
and the man shall release it in the desert.*

Leviticus 16:22

Look up the word *scapegoat* in the dictionary, and you'll read about "a person made to bear the blame for others or to suffer in their place." The word is based on an ancient religious practice of the Jewish people described in Leviticus 16.

Once a year, on the Day of Atonement (Yom Kippur), the high priest selected two goats. He killed one as a sin offering for the nation. Then, according to the Lord's instructions, the priest was to "lay both hands on the head of the live goat and confess over it all the wickedness and rebellion of the Israelites—all their sins—and put them on the goat's head. He shall send the goat away into the desert in the care of a man appointed for the task. The goat will carry on itself all their sins to a solitary place" (Leviticus 16:21–22).

This powerful symbolism was designed to help the people understand that God could continue to accept and bless them as His people only if they confessed and atoned for their sins. The slaughtered goat foreshadowed the coming

work of Christ and His substitutionary death for the forgiveness of sins (Israel's and yours and mine), while the
living goat illustrated God's complete removal of Israel's
sin so that it no longer remained in the camp. The apostle
Peter almost certainly had this atonement ritual in mind
when he wrote that Jesus "himself bore our sins in his
body" (1 Peter 2:24), while David may have pondered it
centuries earlier when he wrote, "As far as the east is from
the west, so far has he removed our transgressions from
us" (Psalm 103:12).

The term *scapegoat* comes from the Hebrew term, *azazel*,
a combination of *az* ("goat") and *azel* (from a verb that
means "go away")—in other words, the "escape goat."
Unfortunately, we've lost this rich understanding of the
word. It has come to mean someone we blame for our troubles or even for our own mistakes and wrongdoings. We
identify those we can blame, lay the fault at their feet, and
then walk away feeling better about ourselves—even
though we have solved nothing.

Have you ever been a scapegoat? If so, it doesn't feel
very good, does it? Most of the time it feels desperately
unfair because you know that you are not 100 percent
responsible for all that went wrong. Maybe you're unfairly
bearing the full responsibility for some situation right now
. . . and it hurts.

Or perhaps rather than being a scapegoat for other people, you tend to look for people to be your scapegoat. You
don't want to feel any guilt, so you seek someone to whom
you can assign responsibility, someone who can bear away
the fault and allow you to escape.

While the ancient ritual of the scapegoat had a legitimate
function in the Jewish community—and it powerfully illustrated all that God would do to free His people from their
guilt and shame—the modern idea of a scapegoat suggests
an unhealthy escape from personal responsibility. The

Hebrew ceremony pictured God's complete and total forgiveness; the contemporary practice actually makes forgiveness harder. The symbolic Old Testament events illustrated a greater spiritual truth; the current practice tries to foist guilt and responsibility upon someone else so we can avoid personal liability.

If you want to grow in your relationship with God and mature in your spiritual life, however, you must reject the modern habit of finding a scapegoat for your troubles. Owning up to the part you have played in some unpleasant event is a major step toward adopting a lifestyle of forgiveness.

TAKE TIME TO PONDER

1. Do you see certain circumstances in your life as someone else's fault? Explain.
2. Why would taking responsibility for your current situation, rather than blaming someone else, improve your situation?

TAKE TIME TO PRAY

Father, thank You for sending Jesus to be my "escape goat," so that through faith in Him I can walk with You in freedom and joy. Teach me how to avoid blaming others for my situation. Instead, empower me to forgive people who have hurt me or complicated my life so that I can move forward in You. In Jesus' name, amen.

INSIGHT 14

THE PLANKS AND SAWDUST
OF SIN

Do not judge, or you too will be judged.
Matthew 7:1

I have discovered a terrible truth about myself: the thing that bothers me the most in someone else is almost always evident in my own character as well. So when I judge what annoys me in another person, I am in fact condemning myself.

This uncomfortable observation aligns quite well with what my mother used to tell me: "Remember, whenever you point your finger at someone else, you have three other fingers pointing back at you." We don't have to look far to see many illustrations of this truth.

Not too long ago, for instance, this country watched raptly as several famous televangelists spoke out harshly against the immorality of this world—only to be caught in their own adulterous affairs.

Another example. It used to bug me to see my daughter get so easily distracted from her immediate responsibilities. "Stay focused and get the job finished!" I would say, feeling a bit of pride in my wise, fatherly advice and believing that I was preparing my daughter for the real world. But then my wife identified several of my projects in various stages of completion. When she said, "Stay focused and get the job done," I got the point.

Every time we judge someone else, we open ourselves to being judged and found wanting *for the same thing.*

Aware of this natural human tendency, Jesus commanded us to turn the microscope on our own sin instead of pulling out a telescope to look at someone else's. When we obey this command, we are much more likely to see the problem in ourselves and to not spend as much time judging others.

Consider Jesus' question: "How can you say to your brother, 'Let me take the speck out of your eye,' when all the time there is a plank in your own eye?" (Matthew 7:4). Acknowledging our plank keeps us from criticizing the speck of sawdust in our brother's eye.

We also do well to realize that, when one of our sins looks very small, it often doesn't seem so ugly; in fact, it can actually be attractive. We may, for instance, consider a little white lie helpful. But when viewed under a powerful microscope, that little lie turns out to be as much a denial of Jesus and His holy character as Peter's threefold denial of Christ in the courtyard of the High Priest's home. When we see our sin for what it actually is—a scorning of God's holy nature, a mockery of His righteous name, and an arrogant declaration that His values and commands make no difference to us—we see our sin as the truly hideous filth that it is.

So, if you struggle with the tendency to judge others, what can you do to change?

The first step is to recognize that *all* sin—yours, mine, and everyone else's—sent Jesus to the cross. All sin is poison. Whether it's arsenic or cyanide, whether it comes in a large dose or a drop at a time, the poison still kills.

Second, if you tend to judge others, then you need to close your mouth, open your eyes, and look in a mirror. Take some time to evaluate your own life, especially any evidence of the offenses you see in others that bother you most. I'm guessing you'll find a plank or two in your eye.

TAKE TIME TO PONDER

1. Have you asked Jesus to forgive the sin in your life? Why or why not?
2. What might happen if you asked Jesus to increase your sense of the sin in your own life so it becomes all the more offensive and undesirable to you? What benefits might you experience when Jesus grants you that sensitivity?

TAKE TIME TO PRAY

Father, thank You for reminding me that all sin—"big" or "small," mine or someone else's—is an ugly stain on the fabric of the universe. Give me eyes to see my own sin first and clearly, so that I am less likely to judge others. In Jesus' name, amen.

INSIGHT 15

WHO WE ARE, NOT MERELY WHAT WE DO

꒰꒱

And forgive us our debts, as we forgive our debtors.
Matthew 6:12 NKJV

Some people think that this verse from the Lord's Prayer teaches that if we don't forgive those who have offended or hurt us, we ourselves cannot be forgiven by God. So these folks feel obligated to forgive immediately even though doing so may prompt great resentment in their heart. After all, it seems deeply unfair that God requires them to forgive a person who may never have said, "I'm sorry."

"Besides, doesn't this verse contradict other things the Bible teaches?" they ask. "God's forgiveness is an unconditional gift of grace and all we need to do is ask for it, so why this condition?"

Part of the answer lies in our understanding of forgiveness. If we think of forgiveness as letting someone off the hook, we will struggle with that apparent injustice. Our offenders may be grateful to be excused, but we struggle that they faced no consequences and acknowledged no guilt. But if we see our extension of forgiveness to other people as an act that transforms our life, then our perspective changes completely, and forgiveness will begin to affect everything we do. Let me explain with an analogy.

Have you ever been around a sports fan who talks about nothing except the big game coming up? Anticipation of that game affects everything the person does. Bring up sandwiches, and he starts talking about halftime snacks. Mention shopping, and she will make a mental note to buy a T-shirt with her team's logo on it. Sports fans don't do these things to *prove* they are fans; they do them *because* they are fans.

In a similar way, once we see forgiveness not as something we do, but as a way of life, the more easily and freely forgiveness begins to flow out of us. It ceases to be something we have to do, but instead becomes something we habitually do, something that we love to do in part because of all the benefits it offers. Consider these benefits.

"When I am able to resist the temptation to judge others," said Gerald Jampolsky, MD, founder of the International Center for Attitudinal Healing, "I can see them as teachers of forgiveness in my life, reminding me that I can have peace of mind only when I forgive rather than judge."

"A wise man will make haste to forgive," said eighteenth-century writer Samuel Johnson, "because he knows the true value of time, and will not suffer it to pass away in unnecessary pain."

"God forgives us . . . Who am I not to forgive?" asks novelist Alan Paton. Suppose an angel came to you and said, "Today, you can commit any one sin you want without penalty, without consequences, and without creating a record of your offense. It will still be wrong, but neither you nor anyone else will have to pay for it." What would you do?

Some people would say, "Hooray! I've wanted to _____ for the longest time, but I was afraid of the consequences. I want to get started right now!"

Other people would respond very differently. They'd look at the angel, shake their head, and say, "No thanks. What pleasure would I get from doing something that I know wounds the tender heart of the God I love?"

Do you know what makes the difference? The first group looks at godly behavior as something they *have* to do (although they'd rather not), while the second group sees godliness as something they *are*, something they want to be—and they loathe and avoid anything that separates them from God.

When you see forgiveness not as something you have to do, but as something you are, then it has become an expression of your character. Not only are you able to embrace God's forgiveness, but you also look for opportunities to forgive others. And this ability to forgive is something you and your heavenly Father have in common.

TAKE TIME TO PONDER

1. What benefits do you receive when you forgive others? Be specific.
2. Do you think it pleases God when you forgive someone begrudgingly, only because you have to? Explain.

TAKE TIME TO PRAY

Father, what an amazing God You are! You continue to forgive me even though I continue to fall so far short of Jesus' example of forgiveness. Create in me a forgiving spirit, so that I forgive not because I have to, but because as I become more and more like You, I want to. In Jesus' name, amen.

INSIGHT 16

THE PRODIGAL'S PATH
OF FORGIVENESS

꧁꧂

When he came to his senses, he said,
"How many of my father's hired men have food to spare,
and here I am starving to death!
I will set out and go back to my father and say to him:
Father, I have sinned against heaven and against you."

Luke 15:17–18

In Jesus' story of the prodigal son (Luke 15), the father's warm welcome of his returning boy provides us a picture of God's unconditional love for us. But this parable also illustrates the process of forgiveness and serves as a model for walking the path of forgiveness ourselves. Consider these steps of forgiveness as illustrated in the prodigal son's journey back to his father.

1. *The prodigal realized how bad his life had become.* He looked around at his current circumstances and realized that his life had come down to sharing supper with pigs.

2. *He recognized what he had done and took responsibility for his actions.* When he found himself destitute and friendless, he began to stop blaming others for his miserable life and started taking responsibility for his thoughtless actions.

3. *He felt empathy for the hurt he had caused his father.* Up to this point, he had thought only of himself, but he finally started considering the thoughts, feelings, and desires of his loved ones, especially his father.

4. *The prodigal realized that his behavior hurt him most of all.* He saw that, by holding on to his "poor me" attitude, he was mostly hurting himself. By clinging to his status as victim, he victimized himself most of all. Note that he was the only human eating pig slop for supper!

5. *He decided to face his problems.* Drinking and carousing hadn't solved any of his problems; in fact, they worsened his troubles. And, at this point, he chose to face his difficulties rather than run from them.

6. *He began to feel contrite for his actions and took steps toward genuine repentance.* He didn't merely feel sorry for what he had done. He also decided to change the way he was living, to turn around and go in another direction, to repent.

7. *He made the difficult choice to return home and reconcile with his father.* He knew it would not be easy to face his past mistakes, but he began to value relationships more than having a good time or asserting his rights.

8. *He rehearsed what he would say.* He gave a good deal of thought to how he would ask his father for forgiveness. His was a contrite and humble spirit; gone was the cocky, arrogant attitude he had displayed just months before.

9. *He allowed hope for a better future to reenter his life.* He had lived in the gutter long enough. But he realized he didn't have to let the mistakes of his past chain him to a terrible present and a worse future. So he let go of what had happened yesterday and instead took steps today to walk boldly into a brighter tomorrow.

10. *He experienced forgiveness from his father.* The prodigal was immediately forgiven and accepted by his father.

When the prodigal son left home, he was filled with resentment: he had concluded that life was unfair because it had not given him what he thought he deserved. So he took unwise steps in an attempt to better his lot in life—and in the process he hurt both himself and those who loved him. Only the choice to walk the path of forgiveness allowed the prodigal to recover from his mistakes and enter a new chapter of his life, a chapter characterized by hope rather than filled with regret.

That same path is available to you. Your heavenly Father is ready to completely and absolutely forgive and accept you.

Take Time to Ponder

1. When, if ever, have you hesitated to return to and reconcile with someone you hurt or harmed? If so, why—and how many months or years have you waited?
2. If this situation is still unresolved, what do you think you should do at this point? What keeps you from taking that step?

Take Time to Pray

Father, I confess that I see a lot of the prodigal in me. I, too, tend to focus on how unfair life has been. I also try to make life fair according to my own terms—and the results haven't been pretty. Forgive me, Lord, and help me go back to those I've hurt and ask for their forgiveness. In Jesus' name, amen.

Insight 17

No Stone Throwing Here

When they kept on questioning him, [Jesus] straightened up
and said to them, "If any one of you is without sin,
let him be the first to throw a stone at her."

John 8:7

Have you noticed that, whenever a crowd gathers on the street, another crowd soon assembles to see what the people in the first crowd are doing? Not everyone hangs around for the same reason; many have no clue why they stand there. During the apostle Paul's ministry, for instance, an assembly of people "was in confusion: Some were shouting one thing, some another. Most of the people did not even know why they were there" (Acts 19:32). This is exactly what happened one dusty day in Jerusalem when Jesus was in town.

Had you been there, you would have seen a large, raucous crowd. Some in the mob had red, angry faces. Others looked on with great anticipation, wondering what might happen next. And still others, those toward the back of the crowd, kept standing on tiptoe to try to get a glimpse of what was going on.

If you'd had a good view, you would have seen religious leaders pointing their accusing fingers at a disheveled woman who was sprawled on the ground in front of them. You would have easily recognized her as a lady of the night—an obvious sinner. Definitely not someone you would want in your neighborhood or near your kids' school.

You also wouldn't have missed that new, popular preacher who had caused such a stir in the city. This Jesus was remarkable because of His quiet strength, His author-itative voice, and His calm spirit in the midst of human dramas like this one. In fact, you would have found it hard to take your eyes off Him.

The controversy quickly revealed itself. The religious leaders announced that they had caught this woman in the act of adultery, a crime deserving of death. And they demanded to know if Jesus would treat her as she deserved or whether He would ignore the values of contemporary society and synagogue and forgive her.

Those looking on half expected Jesus to deliver some kind of amazing oration, but He didn't. Instead, He stooped low and began silently writing in the sand. You would've felt an uncomfortable shiver spread through the crowd and noticed that, one by one, all of the woman's accusers disappeared from the scene.

What had happened? Could the Teacher's scribblings in the dust have frightened away those pointing their fingers at the adulteress? Had Jesus written out the secret sins of those men—you weren't close enough to see for sure—and, in doing so, revealed how their "righteousness" fell just as flat as hers? One thing you do know: Jesus forgave the woman her sins and charged her to start living a life of purity.

As you ponder this story, in what role do you most nat-urally place yourself? Are you like the religious leaders who demanded that Jesus toe the legal line? Are you like those who were thirsty for a controversy and hungry for some entertaining fireworks? Or are you like those people at the back of the crowd, essentially clueless but desperately wanting in on the action?

Or do you see yourself as the woman sprawled in the dirt?

The truth is, all of us have sinned and fallen short of God's glory (Romans 3:23). Just like the woman, we all need forgiveness. To pretend that some of us do and some don't is a lie. So is pretending that any of us could throw a stone at the accused. Only he who is without sin is allowed to throw rocks at others.

TAKE TIME TO PONDER

1. Think about the woman who had been dragged before Jesus by the religious leaders. What does it feel like to be around someone who thinks he or she is better than you?

2. Do people tend to feel judged or safe and accepted when they're around you? Explain your answer.

TAKE TIME TO PRAY

Father, thank You for showing me that my sins are no smaller or less significant than anyone else's sins. Thank You, too, for sending Your Son, Jesus, to die on the cross for those sins so that, by faith in Him, I can live with You forever. And please help me forgive others just as You have forgiven me. In Jesus' name, amen.

INSIGHT 18

CHOOSING TO FORGIVE

But if serving the LORD seems undesirable to you,
then choose for yourselves this day whom you will serve,
whether the gods your forefathers served beyond the River,
or the gods of the Amorites, in whose land you are living.
But as for me and my household, we will serve the LORD.

Joshua 24:15

Every day—and practically every hour of every day—you make choices. And when you say yes to one thing, you are automatically saying no to something else. Even *not* choosing something is making a choice. So, given that you cannot escape making choices, why not make good choices?

To illustrate how often we make choices without even realizing it, I want you to clasp your hands together and interlock your fingers. Now look down at your hands. Which thumb lies on top? Is it your right thumb or your left? Do you realize that not everyone clasps hands like you just did? At some level—whether you were aware of it or not—you chose which thumb to place on top. And a choice repeated often enough becomes a habit.

Now lace your fingers together so that your other thumb rests on top. Hold it there for a minute. Doesn't that feel awkward? But why should it? Many people clasp their hands exactly like this. But it feels awkward to you because it's not the way you usually do it. It's not your habit.

The same principle holds true with forgiveness. You tend to choose whom to forgive—or not to forgive—based on your previous experience and your interpretation of the wrong that has been done. For example, a person taught that any shading of the truth is a lie will be much more offended when a lie is told than someone who grew up in an environment where it was common to slant the information in order to not hurt feelings. You may not be aware of why you are making these choices to forgive or not forgive, but at some level you are making them.

Wouldn't it be better to make these choices consciously? And wouldn't it be best to make healthy, godly choices?

By the way, just realizing that you *have* choices is good for your health. When you have choices available that will improve your circumstances, your stress level lowers and your health improves. A Yale University study demonstrated that when residents of nursing homes received extra choices, they suffered fewer illnesses. These extra choices included what they wanted to eat for meals and what kind of social activities they could have. More choices translated to better health.

Consider what author Viktor Frankl observed: "We cannot control what exists, but we can control what we think and believe about what exists." In terms of our discussion of forgiveness, you can't control what has happened to you, but you can control the choices you make about forgiving the people involved in those events. The mere recognition that you have choices about whom and when and how you will forgive can improve your life. Then, when you choose to forgive, you put into motion a whole series of events that work together for your ultimate good—for your physical as well as your spiritual health. Just as Joshua chose to serve the Lord (Joshua 24:15), you can choose to follow the ways of the Lord and offer forgiveness to others.

Of course, the choice to forgive implies the choice to *not* forgive. But why would you do that when the person who most benefits from forgiveness is you?

TAKE TIME TO PONDER

1. You may not feel like forgiving, but you always have the ability to choose forgiveness. To help you make the best choice, list the reasons you do not want to forgive and then list the reasons it would be best to forgive.
2. What choices regarding forgiveness will you make today that could change your life forever?

TAKE TIME TO PRAY

Father, thank You for the gift of choice. Thank You that You did not make us robots with no choices at all. Help me to remember to both value this great gift and use it wisely for Your glory, for the benefit of others, and for my own spiritual and physical health. In Jesus' name, amen.

INSIGHT 19

"JUST THIS ONCE"

Now therefore, please forgive my sin only this once,
and entreat the LORD your God,
that He may take away from me this death only.

Exodus 10:17 NKJV

Please forgive this sin of mine just this once." Have you ever prayed such a prayer? When you slip up and have to admit it, you may feel tempted to pray for forgiveness for "just this once."

But do you recognize the hidden implication in such a prayer? You're really saying, "If You will forgive me just this once, I will *never* do it again." God knows otherwise.

The Lord knows that any such human boast, explicit or implied, is groundless. We may make such a promise with the best of intentions, but the fact is we have no power to follow through. Yet our confidence can breed spectacular failure.

Remember the apostle Peter? After the Lord told him that he, like all the other disciples, would desert Him at the hour of His arrest, an offended Peter shook his head defiantly and insisted, "Even if all fall away on account of you, I *never* will. . . . Even if I have to die with you, I will *never* disown you" (Matthew 26:33, 35, emphasis added). You

55

remember how that story turned out, don't you? (See vv. 69–75).

Peter, like all of us at some time, seriously overestimated his abilities. He thought that if he tried hard enough, he could succeed on his own without much (if any) help from God. In doing so he forgot—as you and I do—that the human "spirit is willing, but the flesh is weak" (Matthew 26:41 NASB).

So do you really think that when you ask God to forgive you "just this once," you'll never commit that sin again? Who are you trying to kid?

The Bible declares that all of us have sinned—yes, that includes you and me—and that we do so daily. Solomon insisted that "there is no one who does not sin" (1 Kings 8:46). And the apostle Paul reiterated that "there is no one who does good, not even one" (Romans 3:12). Bottom line, we all stand in constant need of forgiveness from our heavenly Father. Happily for all of us, God is more than willing to forgive any of us who will go to Him with a sincere and repentant heart.

In the Septuagint—the Greek translation of the Hebrew scriptures, completed about two centuries before Christ—the idea of forgiveness is rendered by the words *hileos einai*, meaning "to be merciful, gracious." Another popular Greek term that conveys the idea of forgiveness is *nasa*, which means "carrying" or "taking away." Just like the space agency by the same name (NASA) can hurdle rockets into space, so can forgiveness carry away our sins to the farthest away points in the universe. I like that image of forgiveness. And God carries away our sins for us, not because we promise never to commit a particular sin again, but because He is a God who loves to forgive.

That is why the psalmist said to God, "With you there is forgiveness" (Psalm 130:4). And that is why the apostle John confirmed, "If we confess our sins, he is faithful and just and will forgive us our sins and purify us from all unrighteousness" (1 John 1:9).

I need forgiveness every day, and so do you. So let's agree right now never to come to God asking for forgiveness for some nasty sin "just this once."

And, incidentally, you realize who made that foolish request in Exodus 10:17, don't you? Those proud words came from the lips of the arrogant Pharaoh of Egypt, whose land God devastated in order to force him to set the Israelites free from slavery. "Forgive me just this once," Pharaoh begged—only to sin again just as soon as he experienced a little relief from his troubles.

Don't follow his example. Don't pray for forgiveness "just this once." God and, in your heart, you both know that you'll soon be sinning again. Thankfully, He stands ready to forgive again.

TAKE TIME TO PONDER

1. When do you feel most tempted to bargain with God in this way?
2. We should never intentionally plan on sinning again, but why does knowing that God will be there for you when you do sin give you hope?

TAKE TIME TO PRAY

Father, whenever I try to bargain with You based on an overblown estimate of my own abilities, remind me of my weakness and of Your limitless strength. Keep me from foolish pride in my ability to avoid sin and drive me to Your side, where I will find strength to resist sin as well as life-giving forgiveness. In Jesus' name, amen.

INSIGHT 20

COUNT ON IT

But you are a forgiving God, gracious and compassionate,
slow to anger and abounding in love.

Nehemiah 9:17

If ever there were a true statement about God, this is it. God is indeed willing and able to forgive. He's always been this way, and He always will be.

Go clear back to Moses' time, and you hear the same story. This great leader understood his Lord to be a "compassionate and gracious God, slow to anger, abounding in love and faithfulness, maintaining love to thousands, and forgiving wickedness, rebellion and sin" (Exodus 34:6–7).

Several centuries later, the song had not changed. David, the most illustrious king in ancient Israel's history, wrote, "But you, O Lord, are a compassionate and gracious God, slow to anger, abounding in love and faithfulness" (Psalm 86:15).

Keep traveling down the corridors of time, and you'll hear the prophet Joel declare that God "is gracious and compassionate, slow to anger and abounding in love" (Joel 2:13).

About a hundred years later, the prophet Jonah spoke of "a gracious and compassionate God, slow to anger and abounding in love" (Jonah 4:2). I consider his words especially important because he didn't particularly *like* the fact that God was so loving and forgiving that He even forgave Israel's enemies.

After all, God had sent Jonah to the brutal Assyrian city of Nineveh to proclaim its coming destruction. At first Jonah was hesitant about going, but eventually this reluctant prophet did preach to the Ninevites, the people did repent, and God did forgive them. Jonah would have much preferred a heavenly fireworks display that would have turned the city and its inhabitants to ashes for all the evil they had done. So this unhappy man of God sulked about the fact that God would shower His goodness even upon those who didn't deserve it.

Jonah never stopped to consider, of course, that *none* of us deserves God's goodness. None of us has earned or can earn divine forgiveness. God offers it to us not because we are worthy, but because He is merciful and gracious.

And that's the wonderful truth that Jonah's fellow Jews banked on many years after the prophet had passed from the scene. For a long time God's people stubbornly rejected His guidance, and eventually their sins earned them, as promised, a harsh exile in Babylon. Finally, after seventy difficult years in captivity, the children of Israel started returning to their ruined homeland. Some of them must have wondered, *Has God rejected us forever? Have our many sins caused Him to turn His back on us? Will we ever enjoy His favor again? After all we have done, can He ever forgive us?*

As the dejected exiles surveyed the devastation of their homeland, their hearts must have sunk—but not for long. Ezra the scribe, Nehemiah the governor, and many other faithful Jews soon led everyone in a rousing worship service in which an unchanging truth took center stage: "You are a forgiving God, gracious and compassionate, slow to anger and abounding in love."

You never have to worry about whether God will forgive you. After all, forgiveness is not something God does; it is who He is. It is not a nice act or good deed, but a reflection of His changeless character. So, as long as you go to Him through faith in Jesus and with a repentant heart, you simply need to accept the forgiveness He offers. You can count on it.

TAKE TIME TO PONDER

1. Do you picture God as a heavenly Father who can hardly wait to forgive you when you go to Him in repentance? Why or why not?
2. Explain how God's willingness to forgive you affects your willingness to forgive others.

TAKE TIME TO PRAY

Father, I can never thank You enough for sending Jesus to earth so that, by faith in Him, I can be forgiven of all my sins. I praise You that You are still the same compassionate, loving, and gracious God today that You have always been—and that You will always be. Thank You, Lord! In Jesus' name, amen.

INSIGHT 21

THE WORK ONLY FORGIVENESS CAN DO

🙢

And you, my child, will be called a prophet of the Most High;
for you will go on before the Lord to prepare the way for him,
to give his people the knowledge of salvation
through the forgiveness of their sins.

Luke 1:76–77

I recall the first ball-peen hammer I ever owned. I was just a child when it was given to me, and I practiced my carpentry skills by using it on the new television cabinet in the living room. By the time my mother noticed what I was up to, I had finished my work of art. Mother, of course, saw my efforts as a work of destruction.

When I saw the look of concern on her face, I told her not to worry, and I promised to use the same hammer to pound out the dents I had made. But no matter how hard I tried to make things better, I managed only to make things worse.

When I could not correct my errors, my mother had a choice to make. She could choose to throw me—and my ball-peen hammer—out of the house (which might have been the safer alternative for the rest of our household furniture). But, fortunately, she loved me too much to do that. So instead she chose to forgive me.

61

Now, did her forgiveness give me the green light to continue pounding various other objects in the house in order to complete the interior-decorating project I had begun? Hardly. While my mother's forgiveness covered the damage I had done, it also communicated to me her desire that I not continue my "artistic" work on the furniture. I clearly saw how my pounding gave no pleasure to my mother, whom I loved, and I had no desire to upset her again.

Since that time, although I have done many other things wrong, I have never again pounded on new furniture with a ball-peen hammer. But unfortunately I've used other kinds of "hammers" to make things worse. I have used the sledgehammer of ridicule, the claw hammer of guilt, the club hammer of insult, and the tack hammer of criticism. In addition, I have used all types of verbal and emotional mallets, saws, chisels, axes, and blades to—both intentionally and unintentionally—inflict harm on others. Once I caused the damage, I had absolutely no way to undo it. Forgiveness is the only force in the universe with the power to heal the wounds I have caused others.

And, since you're human, you're in the same situation I am. And it's into that situation that God sent His Son. First, though, He sent John the Baptist to pave the way for the coming of Jesus Christ, and John made it clear that God alone offers salvation from the deadly consequences of our sin. The Lord doesn't wink at sin, let it slide, condone it, or accept it. God cannot simply overlook our wickedness or ignore our evil; He is far too holy for that. Instead, He atones for our sin through the death of His beloved Son, Jesus. Since there is no way to undo the wrong we have done, God's forgiveness—made possible by the death of His sinless Son—remains our only hope.

But back to John the Baptist for a moment. When he was born, his father, the old priest Zechariah, declared that his son would "give his people the knowledge of salvation *through the forgiveness of their sins"* (Luke 1:77, emphasis added). John preached "a baptism of repentance for the forgiveness of sins" (Luke 3:3). And Jesus Christ would make that forgiveness possible by His death and resurrection. Salvation—escape from the corruption of our misshapen souls, freedom from the sinful impulses of our fallen nature, and eternal pardon for the spiritual crimes we have committed that deserve only death—comes only by God's forgiveness.

So consider the damage you have done with your own hammers. Maybe you've tried doing the repair work, too, but the more you pound, the worse the problem gets. Isn't it time you allowed forgiveness to do the work only it can do?

TAKE TIME TO PONDER

1. Have you accepted God's salvation through forgiveness? If so, what difference has it made in your life? If not, why not?
2. When we have been forgiven and we recognize how our wrong actions have negatively affected others, why would we do the same things again?

TAKE TIME TO PRAY

Father, help me recognize more clearly each day the truth that I desperately need Your salvation from the consequences of my sin and that Your forgiveness is the only means to that salvation. Then cause your forgiveness to take such deep root in me that it blossoms and overflows into the lives of those around me as a God-given ability to forgive them. In Jesus' name, amen.

Insight 22

A Sign of Strength

꿍⌇Ꙧ

Now Moses was a very humble man,
more humble than anyone else on the face of the earth.

Numbers 12:3

Most conservative Bible scholars believe that Moses wrote the first five books of the Bible. If so, then it comes as quite a surprise to read the man's commentary on his own character: "Now Moses was a very humble man, more humble than anyone else on the face of the earth." It sounds a lot like Mark Twain's statement that "I am the most humble person I know."

Would a humble person really say that he was "more humble than anyone else on the face of the earth"? Doesn't that seem like a contradiction in terms? Do truly humble people boast about how humble they are? Or do the pundits have it right? "If you think you're humble, then you can be sure you really aren't."

Perhaps our puzzlement about this statement comes from the way we have typically understood humility. To be humble doesn't mean having a low opinion of yourself or habitually downplaying your talents or belittling your accomplishments. Humility simply means that you keep your successes and your failures in balance. You have an accurate picture of who you are, the dimples as well as the warts.

"Do not think of yourself more highly than you ought,"

counseled the apostle Paul, "but rather think of yourself with sober judgment, in accordance with the measure of faith God has given you" (Romans 12:3). There's a huge difference between "consider yourself a nothing" and "do not think of yourself more highly than you ought." Humble people not only know who they are and what they can do but also who they are not and where they struggle and fail.

Take Moses, for example. When God first called him to lead the Israelites out of slavery in Egypt, his response may have appeared humble, but in the end it was nothing more than excuse making. For what sounded like humility—he bad-mouthed his ability to lead, his skills as a public speaker, and his ability to fulfill God's call, and then he concluded his argument with, "O Lord, please send someone else"—was nothing more than a revelation of Moses' fear.

We witness evidence of a significant transformation in his character just a few years later. In the desert after Moses had led the children of Israel out of Egypt, the Lord "took of the Spirit that was on [Moses] and put the Spirit on the seventy elders," who prophesied publicly (Numbers 11:25). At the same time, two elders not at the meeting site also experienced the coming of the Spirit and began prophesying—an event that prompted an impetuous young Joshua to say, "Moses, my lord, stop them!" And how did the now truly humble Moses reply? "Are you jealous for my sake?" he asked Joshua. "I wish that all the LORD's people were prophets and that the LORD would put his Spirit on them!" (vv. 28–29). Moses now understood both who he was and who he was not, so he had no fear of someone else eclipsing his star.

Humility is not an endless focus on your wrongs and on what you are incapable of doing, but rather a realistic assessment of your capabilities—no more or no less. This type of humility is far from a weakness. It is, in fact, a real strength. And it is a strength you will need to do the hard work of forgiving. In fact, Mahatma Gandhi once said, "The weak can never forgive. Forgiveness is the attribute of the strong."

So, if you want to get better at extending forgiveness to others, start by developing a humble heart. Accept your limitations. Take responsibility for your mistakes. Apologize for the wrongs you have done. Graciously receive correction and feedback. Think and speak good things of others and rejoice over their successes. Treat everyone with respect. See yourself as a servant of something greater than yourself. And, to maintain a realistic and therefore humble perspective of yourself, keep your eyes on God.

Do these things and you'll be amazed at how much easier it is to forgive.

TAKE TIME TO PONDER

1. Do you think of yourself as a humble person? Do you believe others think of you in this way? Why or why not?
2. Why can fostering an attitude of humility help you become a more forgiving person?

TAKE TIME TO PRAY

Father, I want forgiveness to become a regular part of my life. I want it to be something I am, part of my character, rather than just something I do. Help me become more like Jesus, who "humbled himself and became obedient to death—even death on a cross" [Philippians 2:8]. In Jesus' name, amen.

DOING WHAT DOESN'T COME NATURALLY

꿋꿎ꑚ

If my people, who are called by my name, will humble themselves and pray and seek my face and turn from their wicked ways, then will I hear from heaven and will forgive their sin and will heal their land.

2 Chronicles 7:14

Read again those encouraging words from 2 Chronicles 7. God says He will forgive us when we humble ourselves.

But wait a minute! Is God telling us that we have to earn His forgiveness by becoming humble? Certainly not, for the Bible repeatedly makes it clear that forgiveness is a gift of God. In Romans 6:23, for instance, we read that "the wages of sin is death, but the gift of God is eternal life in Christ Jesus our Lord." In Ephesians 2:8–9, Paul teaches us that "it is by grace you have been saved, through faith— and this not from yourselves, it is the gift of God—not by works, so that no one can boast." So if God doesn't mean that we earn salvation by being humble, then what does this verse mean?

I believe 2 Chronicles 7:14 simply points out that, if we aren't truly humble, we will never seek forgiveness. When we are humble, we'll find it is easier to ask and even extend forgiveness. In fact, it may not even be possible for us to forgive if we remain proud and refuse to see all that is wrong in our own life. Humility also makes us realize that we need forgiveness. Let me illustrate this idea with a story from my own past.

I was a very competitive young man who played hard and always played to win. If people felt run over by my zeal, that was their problem. If they wanted to feel better, they needed to try harder. *Life is tough,* I thought, *and only the strong survive.* And it never occurred to me to ask forgiveness for the hurt and damage I caused by my aggressiveness.

But as I grew as a Christian, I began to see how my competitive spirit led me to leave some people out and to trample others. Only when I started to realize that my actions hurt people—oftentimes, innocent people—did I start to change. I was humbled as I saw that some of my choices had wounded others, and at last I recognized my need for forgiveness. Humility served as a doorway to forgiveness—to being able to both ask for it and extend it.

This is one reason why I believe forgiveness grows best in the rich soil of humility. Some people struggle for a long time with whether they will forgive, primarily because they try to grow the ability to forgive in the dry, nutrient-poor soil of their self-centered hearts. They want to forgive, they may even try to forgive, but they fail over and over again because they just can't get past the awful thing that person did.

Humility, however, helps us take the focus off ourselves as victims and instead remember the times we ourselves were the offender. This perspective reminds us that we, too, need forgiveness; that we, too, have received forgiveness; and that we, too, yearn for others to forgive us when we hurt them. Humility also asks the question, "How could I withhold forgiveness when God and others have so graciously forgiven me?"

If the garden of your own heart is home to too few blossoms of forgiveness, you may not have pursued humility as earnestly as necessary. And don't kid yourself! If you want humility to mark your character, you have no choice but to pursue it, seek it, deliberately go after it, and then cultivate it.

Forgiving others, asking for forgiveness, and having a humble heart—none of this comes naturally. But, by God's grace, all of this can become a permanent part of our character.

TAKE TIME TO PONDER

1. What are some practical ways you can "consider others better than" yourself? Be specific—and choose one option to act on today.
2. Who's the most humble person you know? What does it feel like to be around this person?

TAKE TIME TO PRAY

Father, show me some effective ways I can pursue humility in my life. Reveal to me—ideally before I speak or act wrongly—those times when I don't act humbly. And transform me into a person of true humility. Then help me walk the path of forgiveness that is paved by humility. In Jesus' name, amen.

INSIGHT 24

KEEP YOUR EYES ON GOD

❧

He has showed you, O man, what is good.
And what does the LORD require of you?
To act justly and to love mercy and to walk humbly with your God.

Micah 6:8

Since humility paves the way for forgiveness, it's easy to understand why forgiveness often seems in such short supply. Too many of us have adopted the attitude made famous by Muhammad Ali several decades ago: "It's hard to be humble when you're as great as I am."

Without walking on the correct pathway (humility), it's hard to reach the desired destination (forgiveness).

So what can you do to develop a genuine sense of humility once you recognize a shortage of it in your own life? In my forgiveness seminars, I ask participants to recall all the times they've needed forgiveness. I remind them that they're not perfect and that they've been the offender as well as the offended. Recalling our own shortcomings can go a long way in nurturing genuine humility.

In my seminars, however, I generally don't focus on one very powerful way to grow humility. Since many people in my audience consider themselves completely secular, I don't teach the discipline of meditating on the awesome greatness of God. But if you're a Christian and you want to grow humility in your life, one of the best ways to do so is to spend some extended time dwelling on the majesty, power, and glory of God. Consider just a few texts that speak of God's grandeur:

> How awesome is the Lord Most High,
>> the great King over all the earth! (Psalm 47:2)

> For the LORD is the great God,
>> the great King above all gods.
> In his hand are the depths of the earth,
>> and the mountain peaks belong to him.
> The sea is his, for he made it,
>> and his hands formed the dry land.

> Come, let us bow down in worship,
>> let us kneel before the LORD our Maker. (Psalm 95:3–6)

We can get so wrapped up in our own problems and in the injuries that others have caused us that we don't look beyond our own little world. Humility tends to shatter such self-centeredness. Consider what happens when, even in the middle of our troubles, we follow Job's example and open our eyes to the *bigness* of God: "My ears had heard of you but now my eyes have seen you. Therefore I despise myself and repent in dust and ashes" (Job 42:5–6). There's no whisper of "I'm so great" in those verses!

But when we fill our eyes with painful visions of those who hurt us, we tend to push God completely out of the picture. And that's never a good idea, as God Himself reminds us:

> I, even I, am he who comforts you.
>> Who are you that you fear mortal men,
>> the sons of men, who are but grass,

that you forget the LORD your Maker,
who stretched out the heavens
and laid the foundations of the earth,
that you live in constant terror every day
because of the wrath of the oppressor,
who is bent on destruction? (Isaiah 51:12–13)

If you want to be a forgiving person, then cultivate humility in the deepest part of your being. Do so by meditating on God's splendor, His holiness, His glory, His infinite goodness. When you ponder the greatness of God—"'For I am a great king,' says the LORD Almighty, 'and my name is to be feared among the nations'" (Malachi 1:14)—you will humbly recognize your own limitations and your own sin. You will then find it much easier to forgive those who deal with limitations and sin just as you do.

TAKE TIME TO PONDER

1. Spend a few minutes describing the greatness of God. List some of His attributes.
2. Commit to taking some time every day this week to meditate on the majesty of God. Ask someone to hold you accountable to this exercise and be sure to note the effect of this discipline on your life.

TAKE TIME TO PRAY

Father, I confess that I too often focus on my troubles and on those who hurt me instead of putting my eyes where they really belong: squarely on You. Teach me the true meaning of humility as I meditate on You and Your majesty. Then grow that humble character in my heart. In Jesus' name, amen.

A MANDATORY OPTION

Blessed are the poor in spirit,
for theirs is the kingdom of heaven.

Matthew 5:3

Some things just don't seem to go together. Comedian George Carlin, for instance, points out the strangeness of such word pairs as "jumbo shrimp" and "original copy." Look around and you'll notice lots more—"black light," "civil war," "chili peppers," etc.

I recently heard of a couple who made it clear to a car salesman that, because they wanted to save money, they would decline all optional features. When they found a vehicle they liked, they looked at the window sticker and noted that it had a rear-window wiper listed as an option for an extra two hundred dollars.

"We'd like this car, but without the rear-window wiper," they said.

"Well," the salesman replied, "we try to keep costs as low as possible, but I can't let you have that car without the rear-window wiper. It's a mandatory option in this state."

A "mandatory option"? Some Bible readers feel this same sense of "they just don't go together" when they hear Jesus say, "Blessed are the poor in spirit, for theirs is the kingdom of heaven." Being poor in spirit not only doesn't sound blessed, but it suggests a pretty depressing kingdom of heaven. After all, doesn't the apostle Paul say that the kingdom of God is a matter of "peace and joy in the Holy Spirit" (Romans 14:17)? What does being poor in spirit have to do with peace and joy? Despite appearances, these phrases really do go together—and they do so in the most delightful way.

First, the word *blessed* means to be so specially favored by God that you feel a deep, satisfying happiness that has little to do with merely pleasant circumstances. And that state of being is a very, very good thing.

Second, to be poor in spirit does not mean walking around with a sad face or nurturing a rotten self-image. To be poor in spirit means admitting your spiritual bankruptcy and your constant need to depend on God for everything. Being poor in spirit is the ultimate rejection of self-sufficiency. It is the choice to cultivate a humble heart.

Third, this beatitude differs from all but the last in that it promises a present blessing rather than a future one. Six beatitudes promise that believers "*will be* comforted," "*will* inherit the earth," or "*will be* filled." This beatitude, however, says that the kingdom of heaven *is* theirs—present tense. The kingdom of heaven already belongs to the poor in spirit.

Although Jesus doesn't mention forgiveness in this beatitude, His words have wonderful implications for people who choose to forgive:

- Being poor in spirit—being humble—is key to our ability to forgive. And the truly humble are not morose; the truly humble are happy in the Lord's goodness regardless of their circumstances—and that is a very, very good way to live.
- Since the poor in spirit lean on God for everything, they don't focus so intently on how someone has

harmed them which then chains them to a painful past. The humble know that God is ultimately in control of what happens in their life.

- True humility not only guarantees a bright future, but it brings a blessing right now. The poor in spirit experience the peace and joy of God's kingdom in the present, no matter what challenges they have faced in the past.

You don't have to choose humility if you don't want to. Jesus will allow you to drive off His lot without making humility part of your driving package. But if you want the tremendous benefits it offers—including how it paves the way for forgiveness—then humility really is a mandatory option.

TAKE TIME TO PONDER

1. Why might praying for those people who have harmed you help you forgive them?
2. Why is it hard to hold a grudge against someone when you choose to include humility in your "option package" for life?

TAKE TIME TO PRAY

Father, I thank You that You have promised to grant me a deep kind of happiness if I choose to make humility part of my life. I want the peace and joy You have to offer, so I ask You to help me be truly poor in spirit, to be genuinely humble. In Jesus' name, amen.

INSIGHT 26

EMPATHY: A KEY TO FORGIVENESS

⌘

Carry each other's burdens, and in this way
you will fulfill the law of Christ.

Galatians 6:2

If ever a man learned to be empathetic, it had to be Dr. Sam Beckett. This hero of an early nineties sci-fi television show called *Quantum Leap* traveled through time in a very strange way. When he jumped from one era to another, he always landed *inside* the body of an individual who was facing some extraordinary challenge. He'd look in a mirror and instead of seeing himself, he'd see someone else—and there was no telling who that person might be.

One time, he leaped into the body of a gorgeous secretary named Samantha Stormer, who in 1961 was dealing with her boss's sexual harassment. Another time, he leaped into 1954 and the body of a mental-health patient who was about to receive a faulty electroshock treatment. And once, Beckett even leaped into the body of an astro-chimp named Bobo, who faced some nasty experiments at the hands of an air force neurologist. This quirky show took the idea of walking in someone else's shoes to a whole new level.

It's too bad that we can't occasionally borrow a bit of *Quantum Leap*'s futuristic technology and step inside the body of a person who has hurt or offended us. This new perspective would almost certainly give us a big boost in our efforts to forgive that person. We would be able to empathize with that person's situation and better understand the thought process that ended up causing us pain.

Along with humility, this kind of *empathy* paves the way for forgiveness. Those of us who learn to empathize with others by understanding what it's like to walk in someone else's shoes usually have a much easier time forgiving our offenders.

Empathy, like forgiveness, also helps us obey God's command to "carry each other's burdens, and in this way you will fulfill the law of Christ" (Galatians 6:2). Let me explain.

The first step in bearing another's burden is to empathize with that person's situation. Empathy is the ability to understand someone else's circumstances and the accompanying feelings and thoughts without actually experiencing them. Instead, you imagine yourself being that person and then answer the question "How would I feel if I were in his/her shoes?"

Empathy is the ability to step outside of yourself and compassionately understand the hurts and struggles of others. When you empathize with someone—even a person who has hurt you—you disengage from your own concerns for a while in order to see life from the vantage point of someone else. By doing so you may begin to understand what might have motivated the behavior that you found so hurtful. This insight makes you better able to forgive, because now you no longer see the person as totally evil. Instead, you see that person as being a lot like you—a flawed human being who sometimes makes bad choices and terrible mistakes.

"But I don't *want* to empathize with that person," you may say. "He's nothing like me at all! I don't want to see what happened from his perspective. I know what he did to me, and I don't need to know his warped point of view on it."

If you feel like this, you may not be ready to offer forgiveness. But when that time comes, you will find it much easier to forgive if you can begin to see the individual who hurt you in a different light—not as someone who is totally evil, but as a person made in God's image (just like you) who sometimes struggles to do the right thing (just as you do).

And that is the value of empathy. Vicariously walking in someone else's shoes tends to change our perspective. Seeing life through someone else's eyes, even if only for a short while, makes it far easier for us to travel the road of forgiveness.

TAKE TIME TO PONDER

1. Explain why empathy can help you to forgive someone who has hurt you.
2. What keeps you from empathizing with those who have wronged you?

TAKE TIME TO PRAY

Father, I need Your help to see from the other person's perspective the situation that caused me so much pain. I still feel hurt, and I don't really want to look at this individual in a more compassionate light—yet I know that this is what You ask of me and that doing so is best for me in the long run. So please help me take this step of faith. In Jesus' name, amen.

INSIGHT 27

A LOVE THAT IS STRONGER
THAN HATE

And be kind to one another, tenderhearted, forgiving one another,
even as God in Christ forgave you.

Ephesians 4:32 NKJV

On April 18, 1942, the sixteenth and final B-25 bomber took off from an American aircraft carrier en route to the Japanese mainland. That's how Lt. Col. James H. "Jimmy" Doolittle began his dangerous raid against Tokyo in the months following Japan's devastating surprise attack on America's Pacific Fleet in Pearl Harbor.

Jacob DeShazer, a farmer-turned-bombardier, had volunteered for this mission, as had all the other airmen involved. His target was some oil storage tanks at Nagoya, about three hundred miles south of Tokyo. He knew this would probably be a one-way trip since none of the planes carried enough fuel to return to the carrier. At best, they hoped they could safely ditch their planes over China after completing their individual missions.

The situation turned out quite differently for many of the men. Eight of Doolittle's volunteers were taken prisoner, including DeShazer. He spent the next forty months in captivity, all but six of those in solitary confinement. Most days he could expect little but cruel torture. And, cloistered away in his tiny cell, this soft-spoken man nurtured a deep hatred for his captors.

Back home, however, his mother prayed for him. When the army mistakenly told her that Jacob had been killed, she replied, "I have word from a higher authority that my son is still alive."

DeShazer had always regarded his parents' Christian faith with skepticism, and the brutal treatment he received as a POW only deepened his doubts about God. But when he watched a fellow prisoner—a devoted Christian—die of starvation, he began to wonder what makes human beings hate one another and whether faith in Christ could really change hatred into love. Almost on cue, the Japanese supplied him with a Bible in English, and on June 8, 1944, he submitted his life to Christ. Long afterward he recalled, "My heart was filled with joy. I wouldn't have traded places with anyone."

Then, about a year after he invited Christ into his life, two totally unexpected surprises came DeShazer's way. First, on August 10, 1945, God revealed to him during prayer that the war would end that day and that he and his fellow prisoners would be released—and within a few hours the United States dropped an atomic bomb on Hiroshima. Then came the second surprise. "God wants me to come back and preach the gospel to these people," he declared to a startled fellow POW.

How could a man who had been so horribly mistreated, who had watched his captors both starve and execute his fellow prisoners, ever stop hating the perpetrators of such evil? There is only one path—that of forgiveness. "My love for the Japanese people was deep and sincere," he said. "I know that it came from God."

After graduating from college back in the United States,

DeShazer returned to Japan and preached the gospel of Christ for thirty years. When he first arrived by ship at the Yokohama docks, thousands of curious Japanese were there to greet him. They were anxious to meet the man who had written a tract called *I Was a Prisoner of Japan* and was now returning to show God's love to the very people who had imprisoned him. During the first six years of his ministry in Japan, DeShazer preached four or five times a day in churches, schools, hospitals, tent meetings, and coal mines. Eventually he helped plant twenty-three churches, including one in Nagoya, the city where his bombs had fallen.

If anyone had reason not to forgive the people who had hurt him, it was Jacob DeShazer. But he chose to live in obedience to the command of Ephesians 4:32 and show kindness, a tender heart, and genuine forgiveness to those who had treated him so cruelly. And by so doing he not only helped many Japanese find forgiveness of sin and eternal life, but he himself enjoyed a taste of heaven on earth.

TAKE TIME TO PONDER

1. Why can empathy help you treat with kindness someone who has wronged you?
2. What would it mean for you to be "tenderhearted" toward those who need your forgiveness? Be specific.

TAKE TIME TO PRAY

Father, what a miracle You performed in the heart of Jacob DeShazer when You turned his hatred for the Japanese into love. Only You can do that! And, Lord, I need You to do it again; this time in my heart. Help me to repay malice with kindness and brutality with tenderheartedness. In Jesus' name, amen.

INSIGHT 28

CHOOSE A BIGGER FRAME

꒰⌒꒱

How shall we picture the kingdom of God?
Mark 4:30 NASB

How you picture an object goes a long way toward determining how you relate to it. If, for example, you regard a lake as cold, dark, full of biting things, and a good place to drown, you probably won't make a habit of going there for long swims. If, on the other hand, you consider lakes cool, beautiful, full of natural wonders and good places to get refreshed, you'll probably visit them often to escape the summer heat.

Jesus knew that, similarly, our mental pictures of the kingdom of heaven would largely determine how we relate to it. If we regard heaven as something distant, vague, and hard to grasp, we will likely put very little effort into making ourselves ready for it. If, on the other hand, we consider heaven a very present, concrete, and easy-to-understand reality, we will be far more likely to expend great effort in preparing ourselves for it.

Not surprisingly, this same principle holds true in your experience of forgiveness. How you picture a painful event in your past goes a long way toward determining whether—and how successfully—you will be able to forgive the one who offended you. To understand how this process works, imagine yourself visiting a frame store.

When you want to choose a picture frame for a favorite painting, you consider not only the color and material of the frame but also its size. The smaller the frame, the more your eye focuses upon a particular aspect of the total picture. The larger the frame, the more your eye can take in of the entire scene.

Now suppose you had a painting of an intrepid little bird that had built its nest in the stone hollow of a mighty waterfall. By choosing a small frame with a wide mat, you might highlight only the bird and its nest—a nice enough picture but not very interesting. If, however, you chose a large frame with a narrow mat, viewers would see an intriguing picture of the peace that is possible even in the midst of thunderous commotion.

Clearly, how you frame a picture changes the meaning of the picture. Therefore, to be properly understood, every situation must be properly framed. A very small frame can exaggerate a problem, for it lets you see only the problem. A larger frame, however, allows you to see more of the picture and many critical details left out by the smaller frame. A larger frame allows you to see both good things and bad things in a given scene; a larger frame offers a more accurate picture of how life really is.

Just as framing a picture changes the meaning of that picture, so does the way we frame the experiences of our life. Think about it. When you recall how someone hurt you, what part of the picture does your frame highlight? Do you take in the whole context, or do you focus on only the negative and painful parts of the story? Remember, the larger your frame, the more complete the picture and the more accurate your story will be.

Most of our "big" problems feel overwhelming to us because we have chosen a very small frame for them. We have narrowed our focus to include only hurtful and negative elements. In terms of the illustration above, we have used such a small frame that we see only a single frayed feather lying on a cold, wet stone. The bird is gone. The waterfall is gone. Peace in the midst of turmoil is totally gone. We see only a lifeless scrap of wing decaying in a cold, dark puddle. And it's pretty hard to find any hope *there*.

Think once more about the person who hurt you. What size frame have you chosen for the story? If you enlarged your frame, what aspects of the story—what larger picture—would make your perspective on the situation more accurate and therefore less hurtful?

TAKE TIME TO PONDER

1. What do you focus on when you recall a painful experience from the past? As you answer that question, consider the size of the frame you're using.
2. Explain why a larger frame can take much of the sting out of a painful story.

TAKE TIME TO PRAY

Father, I know that when You look at me, You use a very large frame: You picture me, a sinner, as a believer who stands forgiven and cleansed and righteous in Christ. That means that, in many ways, You see me as You see Christ. I want to follow Your example, so please help me be a "big frame" person, especially when I'm thinking of the painful events of my past. In Jesus' name, amen.

INSIGHT 29

PEACE AND REST—AND FORGIVENESS

~⟨⟩~

He makes me lie down in green pastures,
he leads me beside quiet waters.

Psalm 23:2

To a generation growing up with nonstop, heart-pounding video games, green pastures and quiet waters may not sound very exciting. Gamers tend to want constant stimulation and high levels of noise—and the more frenetic, the better. Quiet can feel uncomfortable, even frightening, to them.

For me, however, nothing feels better than getting away from it all. My favorite vacations involve heading north to put my canoe into the cool, quiet waters of Canada for an entire telephone-free week. The quiet and solitude I experience in that setting always renews my soul. I especially look forward to the haunting calls of the loons. When their sweet, strange song reaches my ears, I've reached the highlight of my day. I feel totally relaxed—physically, mentally, emotionally—and I can almost sense the stress gently flowing out of my toes and into the lake, causing absolutely no ripples as it leaves my body.

Medical science assures us that quieting the nervous system like this not only feels good but also improves our health. The body simply can't go at breakneck speed twenty-four hours a day, seven days a week. It has to get some rest—and the same is true for the mind.

Here's another supporting argument for making time to rest. We live our lives in cycles, alternating between stress and recovery. Tension depletes energy. Relaxation releases tension and allows for the rebuilding of tissue, which gives us more energy and strength to invest in life. People who choose to live continually in stress do not benefit from the recovery phase of this cycle and soon deplete their inner reserves.

A friend of mine once accompanied two bike riders who wanted to pedal across America in just five weeks. Neither rider had ever done anything like this, and although they had spent several weeks training for their marathon trip, it would be a totally new experience for both of them. (My friend rode along in a support van.)

The adventure went very smoothly during the first several weeks. The lead biker set the pace and determined when to start riding each day and when to finish. He had mapped out his route and had a pretty good idea of where he wanted to eat each meal and stay each night. There was a problem, however. His hard-driving personality compelled him to schedule no days off; he intended to bike the three thousand miles straight through without taking a significant break.

And he almost made it. But a few hundred miles short of his goal, his body started wearing out. It just couldn't stand up under the constant stress. He ended up taking one day off, then another couple, then a few more. In the end, he reached his goal more than a week behind schedule—and later than he would have had he taken off one day every seven. There's a lesson to be learned here.

Our high-pressure culture may not highly value peace and rest and relaxation, but they are nevertheless essential to our physical and mental well-being. Would it surprise you to learn that they're also essential to the process of forgiveness? The truth is, an agitated, exhausted, frenetic mind has a great deal of trouble focusing on the task of forgiveness, a task that can be very hard work.

If you are constantly under stress, if you always feel tension in your neck, your back, your shoulders, and elsewhere, then you will probably have a very hard time finding the energy necessary to forgive someone who has hurt you. If that sentence describes you, I have some simple advice: *get some rest!*

Find those green pastures and quiet waters—wherever and whatever they may be for you—and spend some time there. Forgiveness comes more easily when you aren't stressed.

TAKE TIME TO PONDER

1. What benefits could you receive from regularly finding a few quiet moments for yourself? Be specific.
2. What will you do to still your soul today?

TAKE TIME TO PRAY

Father, I marvel at the green pastures and quiet waters You provide for me. Forgive me when I don't take time to enjoy them—and thank You that You "make" me lie down when I need to! Help me, though, to choose to take the rest I need, for my own sake as well as for the benefit of those I need to forgive. In Jesus' name, amen.

THE EXHILARATION OF ACCELERATION

꧂

Be still, and know that I am God.
Psalm 46:10

I admit it. Despite what you just read in the preceding devotional, I'm an adrenaline junkie. For me, the higher the roller coaster, the better. The faster the ski run, the more I like it. And I love to get my heart pounding, my pulse racing, as I lean into the curves on my motorcycle.

There's just something addictive about the rush that comes from . . . well, rushing. I'm one of those guys who would rather burn out than rust out. And when someone tells me, "Hey, speed kills," my reaction is an unspoken, *Maybe, but I would rather enjoy life than die of boredom.*

Speed also tends to give me a sense of power, the feeling of living on the edge, a surge of excitement that opens my eyes to the wondrous gift of the moment. I call it "the exhilaration of acceleration." At times I simply need to be "on the edge" to feel challenged by and engaged in life.

In short spurts, many people enjoy the exhilaration of acceleration. But a lifestyle of running at warp speed creates more exhaustion than excitement. (Yes, I love monster roller coasters, but I wouldn't want to spend a lifetime on one.) Speed works well to break up the monotony of sameness that can clamp its vice grip on our days. But, if we let it, speed can become an adrenaline addiction.

Jesus kept a very busy schedule and often worked from sunup to sundown, but He also carefully guarded His times of rest. And He made sure His followers got the time off they needed. The Gospel of Mark tells us that once, "because so many people were coming and going that [His disciples] did not even have a chance to eat, [Jesus] said to them, 'Come with me by yourselves to a quiet place and get some rest'" (6:31). Similarly, Luke reported that "news about [Jesus] spread all the more, so that crowds of people came to hear him and to be healed of their sicknesses. But Jesus often withdrew to lonely places and prayed" (5:15–16).

Jesus was simply living out the command of Psalm 46:10—"Be still, and know that I am God." In other contexts, the Hebrew word translated "still" (*raphah*) can mean "sink," "to let drop," or "relax." It speaks of consciously slowing down, of stepping off the treadmill, taking a break, and spending some quiet, uninterrupted time with the King of the universe.

A rush of adrenaline can be a lot of fun, but it's not going to help you know that God is God. In fact, the problem with monster roller coasters is that they can be so much fun that we take our eyes off the Lord and instead fix them on His amazing creation. It's fun to celebrate the gift but never at the expense of ignoring the Giver. If He wanted to, God could light up the skies every moment of every day with extraordinary demonstrations of His power and wisdom, demonstrations that would force us to acknowledge Him in all His power and glory and goodness. Surely He could, but He doesn't. He prefers to be known in the still, quiet times, in those moments when He can speak softly to our hearts and we can begin to sense, in the silence, just how awesome He really is.

And, once again, what does this have to do with forgiveness? Plenty.

In my experience, those who are best at forgiveness are those who best know their God. And why do they know Him so well? Because they choose to regularly take significant chunks out of their days to spend some quiet, relaxed, unhurried moments alone with their Lord. In those golden moments when they still their minds and calm their hearts, they get to know and love their amazing God in a more profound way. In fact, they become more like Him. And since He is a forgiving God, they become a more forgiving child of God.

So be still . . . and, in the quiet presence of God, let His forgiving Spirit shape you.

TAKE TIME TO PONDER

1. When was the last time you deliberately chose to be still and know that He is God? In what way(s) were you blessed and encouraged?
2. What would you need to do to include more quiet moments in your schedule?

TAKE TIME TO PRAY

Father, I really do want to become more like You. I want to be a more forgiving child of God, even as You are an amazingly forgiving Lord. Please help me deliberately carve out extended times to be alone with You. And, in those moments, bring me closer to Your heart. In Jesus' name, amen.

INSIGHT 31

LOOK AND BE SAVED

Look, the Lamb of God, who takes away the sin of the world!
John 1:29

Although he died almost twenty centuries ago, John the Baptist continues to remind us that we find forgiveness by turning to Christ. "Look!" John says from the pages of the New Testament. "If you want your sins taken away—if you want forgiveness—then *look!*"

Now consider what it means to look. First of all, we notice particular things when we want to see them. When I was a child, for example, my favorite car was the Corvette, and I spotted them wherever we went. I had trained my eyes to notice them on the road. I could visit any parking lot, and even if a thousand cars surrounded a single Corvette, I would see the 'Vette immediately and not even notice the other 999 wrecks. To my eyes, they were merely white, brown, blue, or red junkers interfering with my view of the Corvette. I wanted to see Corvettes, so that's what I saw.

Similarly, we tend to notice things we may have missed before once we start taking an interest in them. For example, before I bought my first Volkswagen Rabbit, I hardly ever saw one on the road. I even doubted whether many of

91

them existed. But how quickly that changed once I bought one! Then I saw them wherever I went.

This same phenomenon happens with a tune. Once it gets into your head, you begin to recall it all the time. Long ago, for instance, I learned a campfire song called "The Bear Song." It's cute, but it goes on and on forever. Well, when my wife and our daughter and I decided to go on vacation with some friends, their daughter decided to ride with us at one point. Naturally, we sang "The Bear Song" to pass the time. Big mistake! For the rest of the weekend, we all went crazy hearing the children sing "The Bear Song" morning, noon, and night. They simply could not get that song out of their little heads.

Do you know that the same thing can happen in your relationship with Christ? The more you think of Him—the more you really *look*—the more you will begin to notice Him. People who never focus on Christ fail to see His work all around them. But once you know Christ and really look for Him, you begin to see evidence of His presence all over the place. Also, the better you know Jesus, the more His saving grace affects you. You realize just how forgiving He is, so you accept the forgiveness He offers and invite Him to take away your sins. That is how we are saved from the separation from God—now and for eternity—that is the consequence of our sin.

Now consider for a moment how the great English preacher Charles H. Spurgeon was saved by looking. When he was a young man, he visited a Primitive Methodist Chapel in Colchester. The falling snow kept the regular preacher away, so Spurgeon found himself forced to listen to "a very thin-looking man . . . very stupid" who preached from the King James text of Isaiah 45:22—"Look unto me, and be ye saved, all the ends of the earth." The man began, "My dear friends, this is a very simple text indeed. It says, 'Look.' Now lookin' don't take a deal of pains. It ain't liftin' your foot or your finger; it is just, 'Look.' Well, a man needn't go to college to learn to look. You may be the biggest fool, and yet you can look."

The man went on like this for several minutes until finally he cast his eye upon Spurgeon and bellowed, "Young man, you look very miserable, and you always will be miserable—miserable in life, and miserable in death—if you don't obey my text; but if you obey now, at this moment, you will be saved. Young man, look to Jesus Christ. Look! Look! Look! You have nothin' to do but to look and live." Spurgeon looked, and Spurgeon lived.[i]

What are you looking at today? I strongly encourage you to start the day with Jesus. If you do, you'll be surprised at all the places you'll notice Him throughout the day.

TAKE TIME TO PONDER

1. What do you spend most of your days looking for?
2. What might happen if you spent the next few days looking for Christ? Who will you ask to hold you accountable to this experiment?

TAKE TIME TO PRAY

Father, I want to see Jesus more clearly so I can grasp His forgiveness more completely. So please help me to look. Train me to fix my eyes on Your Son. Give me clarity of vision as I look for Jesus all around me—at home, at work, in the neighborhood, even in the car—and then please use what I see to transform me into His likeness. In Jesus' name, amen.

[i] Charles H. Spurgeon, *The Autobiography of Charles H. Spurgeon* (New York: Fleming H. Revell Co., 1898), I:102–104.

A YOKE THAT BRINGS REST

Come to me, all you who are weary and burdened,
and I will give you rest.
Take my yoke upon you and learn from me, for I am gentle
and humble in heart,
and you will find rest for your souls.

Matthew 11:28–29

Have you ever watched an infant or toddler reach the point of total exhaustion yet struggle to stay awake? Maybe it happens at the dinner table, and the little one's heavy eyes blink slowly and her head falls into the bowl of strained vegetables. Or maybe it happens on the living room floor, and his wails of protest at the threat of bedtime are mingled with long seconds of lying crumpled and motionless on the carpet.

Why do our kids so often rebel at the thought of getting the rest they need? They're tired. They're grumpy. They're unhappy. They can barely hold their eyes open—yet they insist (with words or without) that they want to stay up at least as late as we do.

You know what? You and I aren't much different from these kids. Let me explain.

I'm sure you've noticed that life takes a lot of energy. It

can be a real struggle to put bread on the table, build healthy relationships, do the yard work, wash the dishes, balance the checkbook, take care of the grocery shopping, help a neighbor, serve at church, answer e-mail, clip coupons, get loved ones off to school, work, sports, and appointments, etc., etc., etc. Many of us feel exhausted most of the time, and we think we can't slow down or else we won't get everything done that needs to get done.

Wouldn't it be nice if there were someone to lift the burden off your shoulders? Well, there is. I think Jesus looks directly at you and gently says, "Why push yourself so hard when I have a better solution?"

If you feel weary and burdened—especially by your efforts to forgive—know that Jesus invites you to experience His rest. He doesn't mean that He will mysteriously and magically remove the causes of your worries and enable you to walk through life protected by some kind of bulletproof, heaven-made armor. He makes that truth clear when He says, "Take my yoke upon you." After all, a farmer puts yokes on work animals so they can pull heavy loads. So does that mean Jesus is merely asking us to exchange our burdens for His? If so, how would that help us?

Actually, the yoke Jesus refers to here is a picture of discipleship. He is calling you to trust Him, to learn from Him, to follow His lead, and to obey His commands. If you had to do these things in your own strength, your walk with the Lord couldn't help but feel burdensome—and that is why He gives you His Spirit. By tapping into the power of the Spirit, you can take Jesus' yoke upon you, learn from Him, *and* find rest for your soul. He doesn't call you to lounge by the pool but to join Him in His work—including the work of forgiveness—by relying on the Spirit's power. That's the way you can experience both productivity and rest.

So, is the burden of forgiveness weighing you down?

Are you weary from the hard work of forgiveness? Do you long for a respite, for some peace, for some rest for your soul? Then know that Jesus' promise in Matthew 11:28–29 applies to the work of forgiveness as much as it does to any other work He commands us.

And, yes, the hard work of forgiveness is too much for you to bear alone. Jesus offers to take that burden away if you will trust Him with it. The work you need to do in order to forgive will not magically disappear, but His Spirit will bear you up so you can not only survive what's to come but actually thrive in it.

So ask Jesus to be your partner in the labor of forgiveness. Take His yoke of discipleship upon your shoulders. And then feel the weariness melt away as He walks alongside you each step of the way.

TAKE TIME TO PONDER

1. Do you believe that Jesus has a plan for your life and will take care of your needs? Why or why not?
2. What can you do to partner with Jesus in the work of forgiveness so it doesn't make you so weary?

TAKE TIME TO PRAY

Father, I admit that at times I do feel weary. I sometimes feel burdened with the hard work of forgiveness, and I know it's too much for me to bear alone. So I thank You that You don't call me to do this work by myself. Please teach me how to rely on Your Son through His Spirit, so that I will find the help and the rest I so badly need. In Jesus' name, amen.

INSIGHT 33

PEACE FOR THE JOURNEY

*The peace of God, which transcends all understanding,
will guard your hearts and your minds in Christ Jesus.*

Philippians 4:7

Through the ages, this world has seen all kinds of peace.

There was, for instance, the Pax Romana, the Roman peace, that lasted more than two hundred years. From 27 BC to about AD 180, Roman citizens and residents of its provinces led fairly stable and prosperous lives. Unfortunately, the same cannot be said of the empire's enemies. When British tribes revolted against Rome in AD 60, for example, at least 150,000 people died—and then there were those who perished from starvation and massacre after the Roman victory.

There was the Peace of Augsburg in 1555. With that agreement, Lutherans obtained the legal right to exist in the Holy Roman Empire. If you happened to be a Calvinist or an Anabaptist, however, you could still be tried for heresy.

There was the Peace of Westphalia, a collection of treaties culminating in 1648 that together brought the Thirty Years War to an end—a war that erupted in great measure because the Calvinists had been left out of the

Peace of Augsburg. (Some contemporaries called it the "Peace of Exhaustion.")

Today there is the Peace of Maui, a quiet lodge ten minutes from the Kahului Airport on the Hawaiian island of Maui. Of course, to benefit from its peace, you have to book ahead and come prepared to shell out a good amount of cold, hard cash.

The world has always looked for, searched for, and hoped for peace. When I grew up in the sixties, I participated in peace marches almost weekly with my friends and associates. No matter how many peace signs I made, I never seemed to find peace. Not until I put my faith in Jesus did I begin to understand and experience real peace.

Like me on my flower-power peace marches, you may often find peace very elusive on your journey of forgiveness. Even as you work to develop humility and empathy, even as you try hard to give a larger frame to your personal story of hurt, and even as you pray for God's strength to move forward, peace may at times seem very remote to you. What then?

Lasting peace really does come by trusting God rather than by trying to work out everything on your own. Even when we are relying on God, though, we sometimes fail to experience peace as we try to forgive, because we spend too much time worrying about the final outcome. But when we learn to leave the results of our efforts to God and trust Him to use our efforts to accomplish His desires, we no longer have to feel anxious about the final outcome. Jesus already has taken care of that.

In light of that fact, we can obey the command God spoke through Paul in Philippians 4:6–7: "Do not be anxious about anything, but in everything, by prayer and petition, with thanksgiving, present your requests to God. And the peace of God, which transcends all understanding, will guard your hearts and your minds in Christ Jesus." Praying to God is an important step on the journey of forgiveness, but too often we don't pair that step with trust. It's one thing to pray for God's help; it's quite another to hand over our worries to Him and let Him work out the final outcome.

God promises His peace—a peace beyond understanding or expectation—to those of us who will trust Him as we travel the journey of forgiveness, the journey of life. Prayer is key to knowing His peace, but don't forget to add trust.

TAKE TIME TO PONDER

1. What peace have you found this day from knowing Jesus as your Savior and Lord?
2. What practical steps can you take to leave in God's hands the final outcome of your efforts to forgive?

TAKE TIME TO PRAY

Father, I have known moments of Your peace, but I need more than just moments. So please teach me how to trust You for the final outcome of my journey of forgiveness. And help me to do all that You ask me to do—and then to leave the results in Your gracious hands. Taking those steps—in Your grace and power—will help me know more of Your peace. In Jesus' name, amen.

INSIGHT 34

CULTIVATING JOY

≼⌒≽

A cheerful heart is good medicine,
but a crushed spirit dries up the bones.

Proverbs 17:22

As your journey of forgiveness continues, it's important that you stay as positive as possible. I can think of at least two reasons why.

First, a sunny outlook makes hard work—and forgiveness is hard work—far more pleasant and much more likely to succeed. If you set out with a grim determination to forgive, either out of a sheer sense of duty or because you'll feel guilty if you don't forgive, your efforts probably won't get you as far as you want to go.

One pastor shared the following story to illustrate the huge difference between doing a good thing out of joy and doing the same thing out of a sense of obligation. Suppose you're the husband of a lovely woman whom you want to honor on Valentine's Day. You decide to get her a wonderful bouquet of roses and a box of fine chocolates. Seeing you get out of the car with your gifts, she smiles broadly as she opens the front door for you. "Thank you so much!" she exclaims. Then you put the box of chocolates under one arm, hold up your free hand, and say, "Don't mention it.

It's my duty." How effectively would you set the mood for a romantic February 14?

Besides making hard work easier, staying positive contributes to good health. Millions of people have found that humor and joy counteract the negative physical consequences of stress and anger, thus giving your body a chance to recover and even renew itself.

Happiness can do the same for the mind—as I'm sure you've experienced. Think about someone you know who has only negative things to say. Chances are, you don't enjoy spending a lot of time around this person—and, not surprisingly, neither does anyone else. Now think of someone who has a great joy for living. You like being around that person—and so does the crowd standing around him or her. You smile, you laugh, you relax. This person is fun to be around, and you leave for home with a spring in your step.

Actually, you leave with a great deal more than that. The Bible teaches that "a cheerful heart is good medicine" (Proverbs 17:22), and science supports that truth. Happy people, for instance, tend to recover from disease and injury more quickly, more thoroughly, and more often than sourpusses do. Joy has a distinctly positive medical effect on both your body and your mind. If someone could invent a pill that accomplished all the things that happiness does naturally, that person would not only become the richest human being on the planet, but would probably also put a lot of doctors out of work and a lot of hospitals out of business. A positive attitude is *that* important, medically speaking.

That's why it's very important for you to do whatever you can to maintain a cheerful heart as you pursue a lifestyle of forgiveness. After all, as children's writer Isabelle Holland pointed out, "As long as you don't forgive, who and whatever it is will occupy rent-free space in your mind." I would add that, since negative thoughts of how others have wronged you can't possibly bring you much joy, you'd be a lot better off just leaving those thoughts alone. Instead, go for the joy and make the choice to forgive.

TAKE TIME TO PONDER

1. Which option makes more sense—nursing the emotional hurt or being healed? Explain your answer as well as the role of joy in the option you choose.
2. Give two or three examples from your own life when a cheerful heart acted like medicine.

TAKE TIME TO PRAY

Father, I thank You for the gift of laughter and the possibility of having a cheerful heart. Please grant them to me. I want to be someone whom others flock to for the sense of fun I provide and for the happiness they feel in my presence. Help me to exhibit this kind of attitude even as I work on difficult issues of forgiveness in my life. In Jesus' name, amen.

INSIGHT 35

LISTENING FOR GOD'S WHISPER

*The LORD said, "Go out and stand on the mountain in the presence
of the LORD, for the LORD is about to pass by."*
Then a great and powerful wind tore the mountains apart and shat-
tered the rocks before the LORD, but the LORD was not in the wind.
*After the wind there was an earthquake, but the LORD was not in the
earthquake. After the earthquake came a fire, but the LORD was not in
the fire. And after the fire came a gentle whisper.*

1 Kings 19:11–12

If you were God, how do you think you'd normally speak
to the creatures you made? I think I'd opt for the Big Voice:
loud, powerful, reverberating, and just a little frightening.
I'd want to make sure they got my point and scurried to
carry out my instructions. I'd also want my Big Voice to
echo in their mind for a while, to let it soak in that this was
GOD they were hearing from.

That's probably what I'd do, but it's generally not what
God does at all. In fact, the few times where the Bible says
that God spoke in a loud voice, the people who heard Him
usually didn't understand Him or were too terrified to
know what He said.

- When God summoned Moses and the nation of Israel
  to Mount Sinai to receive the Ten Commandments,
  they heard a very loud trumpet blast that kept grow-

ing louder. The people "trembled with fear" and kept their distance. "Speak to us yourself and we will listen," they told Moses. "But do not have God speak to us or we will die" (Exodus 20:18–19).

- During the last week of His earthly ministry, Jesus wanted to glorify the name of His heavenly Father. A loud voice from heaven immediately answered, "I have glorified it, and will glorify it again." Then the Gospel writer reported, "The crowd that was there and heard it said it had thundered; others said an angel had spoken to him" (John 12:27–29).

- As He hung on the cross near death, Jesus "cried out in a loud voice, 'Eloi, Eloi, lama sabachthani?'—which means, 'My God, my God, why have you forsaken me?'" Did the crowd understand? Apparently not. "When some of those standing there heard this, they said, 'He's calling Elijah'" (Matthew 27:46–47).

God actually does us an enormous favor when He speaks to us in a quiet, tender voice rather than in the roar of His omnipotence. Job understood this truth. When he considered the staggering works of God in nature—the stars, the mountains, the seas, the great beasts of prey—he confessed, "And these are but the outer fringe of his works; how faint the whisper we hear of him! Who then can understand the thunder of his power?" (Job 26:14).

The prophet Elijah had to learn this lesson. After a wicked queen treated him unfairly, the prophet ran to a remote place to lick his wounds. There, God startled him with a howling gale, an awesome earthquake, and a ferocious fire—but God did not speak to him through any of these things. When the Lord finally did speak, He used a gentle whisper (see 1 Kings 19:9–12).

Just like Elijah, we hear God speak to us most clearly when we quiet our soul. God desires that we *choose* to listen to Him, not be forced to hear by the sheer volume of

His divine voice.

One good way to quiet your soul is to practice breathing from your belly. Inhaling and exhaling deep, slow breaths prepares you mentally and physically to calm your soul—and it is during this quieting of your soul that you can hear the "still, small voice" of God.

And that's why I doubt it's a coincidence that, in many of the world's languages, the word for "spirit" is the same as the word for "breath." Hebrew for both "spirit" and "breath" is *ruach*. In Greek, it's *pneuma*. In Latin, it's *spiritus*. In Japanese it's *chi*. Take a hint from these languages and learn to use your breathing to quiet your spirit.

Do you want to hear from God, especially what He has to say to you about forgiveness? Then take a deep, slow breath and quiet your soul. Only then will you be ready to hear what He wants to say to you.

TAKE TIME TO PONDER

1. How often do you intentionally quiet your soul in order to hear from God? Describe the steps you take once you're alone with God.
2. Practice taking slow, deep breaths and, as you do, listen to the thoughts that emerge in your head. Listen, too, for the Lord's still, small voice.

TAKE TIME TO PRAY

Father, I want to hear from You; in fact, I need to hear from You. Open my heart to You so that I know when You want to speak into my life—and then open my ears so that I may hear You clearly. Also, please help me slow down and find some quiet moments in every day when I can listen for Your still, small voice. In Jesus' name, amen.

INSIGHT 36

GRATEFUL FOR THE DELAY

๙༼ ༽ C

The LORD is slow to anger.
Numbers 14:18

I tend to keep a pretty full schedule, so from time to time life in my world can get fairly hectic. I find myself rushing from one appointment to another, dashing from one meeting to another, flying from one city to another. Sometimes when this fast pace starts getting to me, I marvel at how fast God can get things done.

Think back to the book of Genesis and how—when God merely spoke a word—into existence popped giraffes and mountains and whales and stars and butterflies and everything else that exists. With a single word! Now that's fast!

And join me in thinking, as I sometimes do when I'm in a plane, of Isaiah's description of one way God likes to travel: "See, the LORD rides on a swift cloud" (19:1). Again, that's fast.

I also remember what the psalmist said about God's view of time: "For a thousand years in your sight are like a day that has just gone by, or like a watch in the night" (90:4). That's really fast compared to my sense of the passing minutes and days and years.

I also like pondering how quickly God can respond to my prayers: "Before they call I will answer; while they are still speaking I will hear" (Isaiah 65:24). And I recall how Daniel's own experience confirms this promise: "while I was still in prayer, Gabriel, the man I had seen in the earlier vision, came to me in swift flight about the time of the evening sacrifice" (Daniel 9:21). Fast!

I know that God can act quickly in judgment too. I think of the time Jesus cursed a fruitless fig tree, and it died in less than a day. "When the disciples saw this," the Gospel of Matthew reports, "they were amazed. 'How did the fig tree wither so quickly?' they asked" (21:20).

While I'm very impressed that God can do things incredibly fast, I am also very grateful that He can also be astonishingly slow. You see, since I tend to mess up a lot, it makes me very happy to remember that "the LORD is slow to anger." That is really, really good news.

Just imagine what would happen if the Lord had a short fuse like many of us do. Where would we be if He let His anger erupt every time we messed up? It would not be pleasant to have an omnipotent God angry with you the first (or second, or third, or fourth, or . . .) time you stepped out of line. So I am very glad and very relieved to hear God Himself say, "For my own name's sake I delay my wrath; for the sake of my praise I hold it back from you, so as not to cut you off" (Isaiah 48:9). And it encourages me to read that God "was merciful; he forgave their iniquities and did not destroy them. Time after time he restrained his anger and did not stir up his full wrath" (Psalm 78:38).

I learn from passages like these that God "delays" and "restrains" His wrath, He "holds it back" from us, and He does not "stir it up" against us. Sin always makes Him angry, but He controls His anger; it does not drive Him to do rash and regrettable things, as our anger often does.

I also learn from these verses that anger is not, in and of

itself, a bad thing. How could it be if the Bible uses words like *anger* and *wrath* and even *fury* to describe God's reaction to human sin? If our pure and perfect God can get angry, then anger can be a righteous, even holy response to evil situations or circumstances.

God does indeed have every right to unleash His anger at us for the evil we do, yet He remains "slow to anger." And that makes me wonder: since we are created to reflect God's glory, then shouldn't we learn how to be "slow to anger"?

TAKE TIME TO PONDER

1. Is it OK for Christians to express anger? Why or why not? And if it is, what are some appropriate ways?
2. What can you do to slow down your anger?

TAKE TIME TO PRAY

Father, I praise You for being a God who is "slow to anger." I know that I have aroused Your anger more times than I realize, and yet, out of love, You have restrained it. Thank You for holding it back from me. And, Lord, I ask now that You would teach me how to follow Your example and, like You, be "slow to anger." In Jesus' name, amen.

Insight 37

A Sure Route to Many Sins

Man's anger does not bring about the righteous life that God desires.
James 1:20

Since God is slow to anger, it makes sense that we should strive to emulate Him in this regard. And, in fact, that's exactly what the apostle James urged us to do: "Everyone should be quick to listen, slow to speak and *slow to become angry*" (1:19, emphasis added).

James also warned that human anger "does not bring about the righteous life that God desires" (v. 20). In other words, our anger often leads to some very nasty scenes. Consider a few stories from Scripture that ended badly because of uncontrolled human anger:

- An angry Cain killed his brother Abel. When God accepted his brother's sacrifice, but not his, "Cain was very angry, and his face was downcast." Because Cain didn't master his anger, he became a murderer (Genesis 4:2–8).
- When Jacob tricked his brother out of the firstborn's blessing, Esau schemed: "The days of mourning for my father are near; then I will kill my brother Jacob." Esau allowed his anger to brew, and Jacob lived only because his mother sent him away from his murder-

ously angry brother (Genesis 27:41–45).

- When King Saul and a young David returned from a successful military campaign, the crowds cheered David more than they did Saul. So "Saul was very angry; this refrain galled him. . . . And from that time on Saul kept a jealous eye on David" (1 Samuel 18:8–9). Saul attempted several times to murder the young warrior.
- When King Ahab unsuccessfully tried to buy a plot of land from a man named Naboth, the spurned king "went home, sullen and angry" and "lay on his bed sulking and refused to eat" (1 Kings 21:4). Eventually his brewing anger led to Naboth's murder.
- When a prophet of God rebuked King Asa for relying on political alliances rather than on God, "Asa was angry with the seer . . . he was so enraged that he put him in prison. At the same time Asa brutally oppressed some of the people" (2 Chronicles 16:10).
- King Uzziah became angry and abusive when eighty courageous priests rebuked him for trying to burn incense in the temple. "While he was raging at the priests in their presence before the incense altar in the LORD's temple, leprosy broke out on his forehead"—a divine judgment (2 Chronicles 26:19).

Anger made King Nebuchadnezzar order the execution of all the wise men of Babylon (Daniel 2:12). Anger drove the prophet Jonah to sulk after God spared the repentant sinners of Nineveh (Jonah 4:1). Anger prompted the older brother in Jesus' parable of the prodigal son to grouse about the treatment he felt was so unfair (Luke 15:28). Anger spurred the Pharisees to condemn Jesus for healing on the Sabbath (John 7:23).

Your anger and mine hardly bring about the righteous life God desires. The book of Proverbs says it very succinctly: "An angry man stirs up dissension, and a hot-tempered one commits many sins" (29:22).

Learning to forgive cools your anger toward the person who hurt you and helps you keep that anger from raging out of control. So rather than trying to swallow your temper, try practicing forgiveness instead. You may be amazed at the results.

TAKE TIME TO PONDER

1. Would the people who know you best describe you as someone who tends to be slow or quick to anger? Support your answer with evidence from your life.
2. Why are forgiveness and resentment mutually exclusive?

TAKE TIME TO PRAY

Father, I don't want my anger to rage out of control and cause the kinds of tragedy that other people's anger has. So please help me deal with my anger by becoming a forgiving person. By Your grace, help me to be "slow to anger," just as You are. In Jesus' name, amen.

INSIGHT 38

A HEART ATTACK'S BEST FRIEND

You have heard that it was said to the people long ago,
"Do not murder, and anyone who murders will be subject to
judgment." But I tell you that anyone who is angry with his brother
will be subject to judgment.

Matthew 5:21–22

Anger kills, and it does so in many ways.

As both the Bible and newspaper headlines attest, anger often leads to murder. In fact, whether the killing is intentional or not, anger is involved in most murders. Road rage kills on the freeways just as surely as an out-of-control argument can escalate into murder at home.

But Jesus taught that, even when anger doesn't trigger a homicide, in God's eyes, it deserves the same judgment as murder itself. In other words, to be angry with someone is as serious as killing that person.

If strong enough, anger can also lead to the death of a friendship and severe emotional damage. Yes, anger can cause both physical and emotional harm.

But did you know that your anger can also destroy you? Many well-designed research studies have shown that anger kills the one who harbors it. That's why modern medicine warns that too many of us get angry more often—and stay angry longer—than is healthy.

In fact, Dr. Redford Williams at Duke University has chillingly demonstrated that anger kills people who won't let it go. In one study, he reviewed the anger scores of 225 physicians who had graduated twenty-five years earlier from medical school. When they first began their medical training, each student had to take a psychological test, part of which measured anger. Dr. Williams arranged these old anger scores from the highest to the lowest and then sent the physicians a questionnaire about their current health.

He discovered that, twenty-five years later, those doctors who had the highest anger scores while in school also had the highest incidences of heart disease and early death. He concluded that a person's level of anger can accurately predict illness, particularly heart disease. His study soon convinced the American Heart Association to declare anger a risk factor for heart disease. And the respected journal *Circulation* warned in 2000 that "a person who is most prone to anger is three times more likely to have a heart attack than someone who is least prone to anger."

People who choose to live in a world of anger and resentment also tend to suffer from such ailments as elevated blood pressure, chronic headaches, fatigue, lower back pain, and even irritable bowel syndrome. When you live with anger, you tie your stomach in knots—and while your tummy might welcome the occasional pretzel, it does not appreciate being turned into one.

While unresolved anger can lead directly to serious health problems, you can reverse its harmful effects by practicing forgiveness. Researcher Fred Luskin demonstrated that teaching people how to forgive can measurably reduce their anger. In another study, Charlotte Witvliet demonstrated that by simply asking people to imagine they had forgiven someone, their health began to improve.

In a study I did on forgiveness, participants with high blood pressure and elevated levels of anger were able to successfully reduce their blood pressure by practicing forgiveness. In addition to this obvious health benefit, they also made comments like "I now have a spiritual awakening in my life. My life now has greater direction and purpose. I feel as though I'm finally getting my life back on track."

The bottom line: forgiveness saves lives. So why not stop the anger before it kills . . . you?

TAKE TIME TO PONDER

1. Will remaining angry at someone who has harmed you make a significant difference in changing your circumstances? Explain.
2. What physical, mental, emotional, and/or relational price are you paying by holding on to your anger?

TAKE TIME TO PRAY

Father, I don't want my anger to kill anyone—whether literally or figuratively, whether others or myself. When I feel like harboring my anger against someone, remind me of Jesus' words in Matthew 5:21 and direct me to instead walk the healing path of forgiveness. In Jesus' name, amen.

INSIGHT 39

THE WORST KIND OF ANGER

You have heard that it was said, "Love your neighbor and hate your enemy." But I tell you: Love your enemies and pray for those who persecute you, that you may be sons of your Father in heaven.

Matthew 5:43–45

When did you last feel really angry? Can you name the time?

Even if you can—and many people can't—I have to tell you that you're probably wrong. Here's why.

Anger wears many disguises, and it comes equipped with many changes of clothing. In other words, you may not always recognize anger for what it is. It's easy to identify anger when you witness a heated exchange of shouting, hurtful allegations, and jabbing fingers. You witness an outburst like that and think, *That's real anger.* And so it is. But it's not the most common way people express their anger. Nor is it the most damaging form of anger.

In fact, the emotion of anger burns at various temperatures. It can be present even if it doesn't make your face turn crimson or cause your veins to pop out of your neck. Anger exists all along the following continuum. The only difference between these stages is intensity:

**Annoyed ⇒ Irritated ⇒ Upset ⇒ Hostile
⇒ Enraged ⇒ Resentful**

"I'm not angry with her," you might say. "I'm merely annoyed." But to be annoyed is to be angry.

"I'm not angry with him," you insist. "I'm just a little upset. That's all." But to be upset is to be angry.

Shakespeare wrote that "a rose by any other name would smell as sweet." It's equally true that anger by any other name is just as destructive—and one type of anger in particular tends to do more damage than the others.

That most destructive villain in the anger family tends to remain submerged just below the surface, and it does its damage without high-decibel scenes. Resentment is the most common form of anger, and it endangers your health more than any of its red-faced cousins.

"Resentment kills a fool," the Bible says straightforwardly (Job 5:2). "The godless in heart harbor resentment," echoes Job 36:13.

Do you resent someone who has caused you harm? Do you harbor a grudge against this person, hoping—however silently—that one day he will "get his" or she will "get hers"? If so, you're feeling angry right now. And remember this: resentment kills—and if you continue to allow it to take up space in your heart, it will kill you.

Jesus understood this, and that's probably one reason why He told us to love our enemies and pray for those who persecute us. "But that isn't natural!" you object. You're right, of course; it's not. And the only way you can love those who hurt you and pray for their welfare (rather than merely hoping for divine retribution) is by allowing Jesus to work in you by His Spirit. Only as Christ is supernaturally formed in you (Galatians 4:19) can you hope to love your enemies and pray for those who persecute you. And how do you do this? The only thing that can drive resentment out of your heart is forgiveness.

By giving up the resentment that can kill you, you can more easily embrace the forgiveness that heals you. Why would anyone turn down such a deal?

TAKE TIME TO PONDER

1. In what ways has resentment damaged some of your relationships? Be specific.
2. What is keeping you from forgiving someone you currently resent? What will you do about that barrier to forgiveness?

TAKE TIME TO PRAY

Father, it's easier for me to admit my red-faced anger than my smoldering resentment. I see now, though, that both come from the same deadly tree and that You call me to deal with them by the power of Your Spirit. Please help me identify, confess, and release my resentment by forgiving my enemies. In Jesus' name, amen.

Insight 40

Don't Let It Stay!

"In your anger do not sin":
Do not let the sun go down while you are still angry.
Ephesians 4:26

The main problem with anger is not its existence, but its tendency to overstay its welcome. As beings created in God's image, we—like God—can rightfully get angry at injustice and unfair treatment. God knows, however, that we have a bad habit of hanging on to our anger—stoking it, feeding it—until it destroys us. That is why God commands, "'In your anger do not sin': Do not let the sun go down while you are still angry."

Notice that He does *not* say, "Don't be angry." Rather, He says, in essence, "There is a time and a place to be angry, but don't let your anger take over your life."

In and of itself, anger is neither good nor bad. It's simply a messenger informing you that something has gone wrong and needs your immediate attention. In fact, God designed anger to serve several helpful functions:

- *Anger helps you face a hurtful situation.* Anger gives you the energy you need to face a situation you might otherwise want to avoid. It provides both the motivation and the strength you need in order to act productively. After scores of children died in auto accidents caused by intoxicated drivers, for example, MADD (Mothers Against Drunk Drivers) took decisive action to curtail the carnage. Its anger-motivated efforts have saved untold thousands of lives.

- *Anger drives you to clarify your goals and overcome barriers to achieving those goals.* Hurt and pain tend to keep you stuck in the past, but anger can motivate you to work for your dreams. Anger energizes you to act, and it fortifies your belief that your actions can make a difference. And if something stands in the way of a good result, your anger can help you courageously address it rather than accept something that is unacceptable.

- *Anger helps you assert yourself.* Some Christians mistake subservience for humility. They don't feel right about asserting themselves even in situations when their failure to do so will prolong their hurt. But the Bible doesn't put a high value on your keeping silent while someone continues to abuse you. Although Jesus told us, "If someone strikes you on the right cheek, turn to him the other also" (Matthew 5:39), He also responded to a slap on the face at His sham trial with a sharp, "If I said something wrong, . . . testify as to what is wrong. But if I spoke the truth, why did you strike me?" (John 18:23). And although the apostle Paul asked some immature Christians, "Why not rather be wronged? Why not rather be cheated?" (1 Corinthians 6:7), he also told someone who ordered him struck, "God will strike you, you whitewashed wall! You sit there to judge me according to the law, yet you yourself violate the law by commanding that I be struck!" (Acts 23:3). Both our Lord and the apostle Paul spoke up against abuse.

- *Anger can lead to a spirited and rewarding life.* The root word for anger originally described the snorting breath of a bull. Anger is energy waiting to act, and when we express it and use it in the right way, anger can lead to a spirited and action-oriented life.

Remember that anger, in and of itself, is not wrong. The Bible tells us that God gets angry; Jesus Himself got angry; and anger is a legitimate part of our own human experience. But "in your anger do not sin." God designed your anger to serve a good and crucial purpose—yet you must not let it overstay its welcome.

Take Time to Ponder

1. Describe a time when your anger actually helped you.
2. What can you do to make sure that you don't remain angry longer than is necessary? Be specific.

Take Time to Pray

Father, teach me to discern when my anger reflects Your holy character and when it only expresses my own sinful, selfish desires. Help me channel my anger for good purposes that please and honor You. Most of all, give me the strength and wisdom to control it so that it doesn't control me. In Jesus' name, amen.

INSIGHT 41

BITTER OR BETTER?

*But Joseph said to them, "Don't be afraid. Am I in the place of God?
You intended to harm me, but God intended it for good to accomplish
what is now being done, the saving of many lives. So then, don't be
afraid. I will provide for you and your children." And he reassured
them and spoke kindly to them.*

Genesis 50:19–21

Some of the most bitter feuds in history involve family
members, and we human beings haven't changed much
through time. Case in point. A few years ago the television
show *48 Hours* did a special on modern-day family feuds.
The following were among the several nasty disputes the
program highlighted:

- Brothers Jeff and Tracy Kirk worked as loggers in
  Unity, Maine (get the irony?). As children and young
  adults, they spent all their time together. Now they
  can only scream at each other, peppering their conversation with words like *scumbag*, *lazy*, and *ignorant*.
  Their feud came to a head after purchasing together a
  piece of logging equipment that each later wanted for
  himself. Court mediation appeared to settle the legal
  aspects of the issue, but the feud goes on. "It's almost
  like it would be easier if it was back in the old West,
  and you could just shoot it out and be done with it,"
  said Tracy.

- Back in 1974, the wealthy Tinney family hired an unlicensed plumber named Kevin Koellisch to do a few repairs on their Newport, Rhode Island, mansion. Soon he moved in, and by 1990 the aging Tinney matriarch, Ruth, adopted Koellisch as her son (he was thirty-seven years old). She died five years later, and soon a fight between Kevin and Ruth's biological son, Donald, erupted over the house and its millions of dollars in antiques. Although they lived in the same house, they communicated only through lawyers and faxes. A judge eventually decided that Kevin had conned the elderly Ruth and had no right to an inheritance, but Kevin appealed the decision. "I will never, ever, in any way forgive him," said Donald. "No matter what. If God asked me, I wouldn't do it."

Such an attitude isn't hard to understand, but it never does anyone any good. You may feel perfectly justified in your choice to withhold forgiveness from someone who hurt you, but by doing so, you actually hurt yourself most of all. So the real question in cases like these is, "Do I want to get better—or bitter?"

If anyone had a right to remain angry with his family members for their abusive treatment, it was our Old Testament friend Joseph. His ten older brothers sold him into slavery and then told their father that a wild animal had killed him. For the next several years, Joseph's service to Potiphar was exemplary, but he nevertheless found himself a slave in prison for a crime he didn't commit (see Genesis 39). And then, through a remarkable sequence of events that only God could have orchestrated, Joseph was not only released from jail, but he became second-in-command of Egypt, the most powerful nation at the time.

At the height of Joseph's power, his destitute brothers straggled into Egypt seeking relief from the terrible drought and famine in Israel. Although Joseph recognized them immediately, they did not recognize him. So Joseph faced a tough choice: would he make his brothers pay for mistreating him? He had the power to do whatever he wanted: he could kill them, enslave them, or jail them. So what would he choose? He did what Donald Tinney of Newport, Rhode Island, said he'd never do: he forgave his brothers. "You intended to harm me," Joseph proclaimed, "but God intended it for good to accomplish what is now being done, the saving of many lives. So then, don't be afraid. I will provide for you and your children."

By forgiving his guilty brothers, Joseph rejected the bitter way and chose a better way to live life. His forgiveness of his brothers benefited the family, but perhaps it benefited Joseph most of all. He freed himself from the debilitating burden of unrelenting resentment against those who had wronged him.

You have the same choice Joseph did. Bitterness or a better life—which are you choosing?

TAKE TIME TO PONDER

1. In what ways—physical, mental, emotional, spiritual—might holding on to a grievance over time hurt you?
2. What would you say to someone who declared, "Under no circumstances, even if God asked, would I forgive that person"?

TAKE TIME TO PRAY

Father, if Joseph could forgive his brothers for their awful mistreatment of him, then through the power of Your Spirit I can certainly forgive those who have wronged me. I choose to become better rather than bitter. In Jesus' name, amen.

INSIGHT 42

FORGIVENESS
AND THE GOLDEN RULE

So in everything, do to others what you would have them do to you,
for this sums up the Law and the Prophets.

Matthew 7:12

A lot of people have had a great deal of fun coming up with their own version of the golden rule. Folks have put their own unique spin on the traditional version of Jesus' famous counsel—"Do unto others as you would have them do unto you."

For instance, the writer's version of the golden rule says, "Do not take more from the works of others than you would have them take from you."

The tennis player's version goes something like this: "Give others more love than they are able to give you." Of course in tennis, love means no score.

According to some, the golden rule of the business world says, "Do unto others before they do unto you."

The cynic's version of the golden rule says, "He who has the gold makes the rules."

You've probably met people who seemed to live according to the last two versions. Too frequently, it seems, we run into people more powerful than we are who like to throw their weight around. They want us to know that they are richer than we are, have more clout than we do, have more important friends than we have, and enjoy more options than we do. Since they have the gold, they insist on making the rules, and at every opportunity they do to us before we would ever think of doing to them.

If you ever find yourself in the crosshairs of such abusive folks, you can basically respond in one of two ways—with revenge or forgiveness. When you choose revenge, you create your own form of justice. The person who hurt you has made your life unfair, so you act to restore a degree of fairness. You replace the golden rule with *lex talionis*, the principle of "an eye for an eye and a tooth for a tooth"—conveniently forgetting that this Old Testament principle was designed to *limit* retribution, not mandate it. Getting revenge may make you *feel* better, at least for a short while, but it never actually *makes* you better. Most of the time, people who seek revenge end up acting like—or even worse than—the ones who hurt them. You see, a spirit of revenge has a nasty way of setting up camp in your heart. It claims squatter's rights.

The other option is forgiveness: *even when someone hurts you*, you decide to treat that person as you wish to be treated. This approach may not always seem fair, and rarely is it easy, but God's powerful Spirit can help you live according to the golden rule. And when you do, you won't become like the people who hurt you and then blame them for making you the person you have become.

Have you noticed that, if we human beings aren't careful, we often become the kind of people we despise? If we ever give in to our baser instincts to seek revenge, we allow the evil of the other person to shape who we are. Then we'll wake up one day, look in the mirror, and see that evil in ourselves.

Living by the golden rule may not seem fair and, again, it's not easy, but—like all of the Lord's laws—it's for your own good. So will it be revenge or will it be forgiveness?

TAKE TIME TO PONDER

1. In what ways did Jesus Himself live by the golden rule? Be specific.
2. Do you more naturally gravitate to an eye for an eye and a tooth for a tooth or to the golden rule? Give an example or two.

TAKE TIME TO PRAY

Father, I thank You that You operate according to the golden rule. Every day of my life, You shower me with grace rather than give me the punishment my sins deserve. Please help me learn from Your example and draw on Your power to live according to the golden rule in my own life. In Jesus' name, amen.

Insight 43

Hope with a Capital *H*

Hope deferred makes the heart sick,
but a longing fulfilled is a tree of life.
Proverbs 13:12

Hope for the future can make a big difference in your health today. As author Norman Cousins put it, "People can live forty days without food, three days without water, fifteen minutes without air—but not one second without hope."

One researcher, in fact, discovered that pessimists suffer from twice as many infectious illnesses and make twice as many visits to the doctor as people who maintain a hopeful outlook on life. Partly in response to accounts like these, Cousins declared, "People tell me not to offer hope unless I know hope to be real, but I don't have the power not to respond to an outstretched hand. I don't know enough to say that hope can't be real. I'm not sure anyone knows enough to deny hope. I have seen too many cases these past ten years when death predictions were delivered from high professional station only to be gloriously refuted by patients for reasons having less to do with tangible biology than with the human spirit, admittedly a vague term but one that may well be the greatest force of all within the human arsenal."

A research project was designed to investigate the protective benefits of hope in the laboratory where conditions could be closely regulated. One group of rats was given a mild, escapable shock; another group a mild, inescapable shock; and the third—the control group—received no shock at all. The rats in the first group could stop the shock by pressing on a bar in the cage. When a rat pressed the bar to stop the shock, the shock also stopped in the cage without a bar. So neither group of rats felt the shock longer than the rats in the other group. The only difference was that the rats with the bar could do something about the shock, whereas the bar-less rats learned helplessness.

Before the experiment, researchers implanted cancer cells into the rats. The dosage was such that, under normal circumstances, 50 percent of the animals would reject the tumor and live while the other 50 percent would succumb to the disease. By the end of the experiment, however, 70 percent of the rats in Group 1 rejected the tumor; in Group 2, only 27 percent rejected the tumor; and in Group 3, 50 percent rejected the tumor, just as expected. The only variable was the psychological state of mind—hope or hopelessness—brought on by the stress of shock and the ability or inability to stop the shocks.

While no experiment done with animals directly relates to the human condition, this experiment does suggest that hopelessness about our ability to impact the negative experiences of life can have negative consequences on our health. In fact, a look at the rats' living tissue under the microscope helps explain how hope can have such an effect. Researchers discovered that the rats' experience of inescapable shock weakened their immune systems. The T-cells—part of a body's immune system—lost the ability to multiply sufficiently to prevent the growth and spread of cancer cells in those rats that had learned helplessness. In other words, researchers discovered that a loss of hope not only affects behavior; it also influences biology.

A chief question for all of us, therefore, ought to be, "What can I do to increase my sense of hope?" Dr. John Harvey Kellogg—one of the country's most famous physicians in his day and the inventor of the cold cereal that bears his family name—once stated, "Belief in God is the basis of all health. Belief gives rise to hope, and hope is one of the most powerful stimulants to which the body can be subjected." Since our God is a forgiving God, I maintain that the fact that we can count on His forgiveness—and on His helping us to forgive—is one of the most powerful hope-stimulators in the universe. When you forgive, you release yourself from a painful past and open the door to an exciting future—and that's actually a good definition of hope!

Former UCLA basketball coach John Wooden was exactly on track when he said, "Things turn out best for the people who make the best of the way things turn out." Forgiveness definitely helps you make the best of the way things turn out—and that translates to hope with a capital *H*.

TAKE TIME TO PONDER

1. Why would a more hopeful outlook improve your own situation? Be specific.
2. What can you do to become a more hopeful person? Which step will you take this week?

TAKE TIME TO PRAY

Father, how glad I am that we can call You "the God of hope," as Paul did in Romans 15:13. Help me see more clearly the connection between hope and forgiveness—and then increase my hope for the future as I practice forgiveness. In Jesus' name, amen.

INSIGHT 44

HEALING FAITH

꒰ ꒱

He said to her, "Daughter, your faith has healed you.
Go in peace and be freed from your suffering."
Mark 5:34

W hy do more heart attacks occur Monday morning than any other time of the week? And why does the usual daily death rate in this country drop nearly 30 percent on Christmas Day?

Does some biological or medical factor explain this statistic? Not that I know of. But I do know that most Americans do not like their work, so they are extra stressed when they return after two days off. And I know that most people don't want to miss Christmas Day, so they somehow will themselves to live. These statistics therefore suggest to me that our beliefs and perceptions about life have a major impact on our health. Our beliefs create well-traveled emotional pathways that, in turn, tend to trigger physiological responses.

You see this relationship between perceptions and health played out every day in hospitals across the country. Two patients suffering from the same illness, for example, arrive on the same day. If one expects a quick recovery, but the other believes the worst is yet to come, the hopeful individual is far more likely to recover before the pessimistic one does. Positive beliefs can nurture a sense of peacefulness, self-confidence, and purpose in life, which in turn can ease one's anxiety and stress. The result? Improved health.

In addition, the well-known placebo effect offers a striking demonstration of the healing power of our belief. As you may know, a placebo is an inert substance with no pharmacological properties—a sugar pill, in most cases. Experts tell us that a placebo can often have more potent effects than an actual medicine. Why? Because when people believe they will be healed because of a pill—regardless of what's in or not in that pill—their hopeful belief can often trigger the healing even if the pharmacology can't.

The placebo effect has long puzzled medical researchers who can no more explain it than dismiss it. Scientific study after scientific study has shown that, for virtually any disease, roughly one-third of the patients will improve when given a placebo. In other words, patients who believe the treatment will help them tend to experience the help they expect.

In addition, many studies also indicate that a drug—or even a placebo—is more effective when the physician who administers it has a strong faith in its effectiveness. In fact, a physician's expectation of a drug's effectiveness can alter the outcome of therapy by 25 to 30 percent for either good or bad, depending on the physician's message of hope or doom.

Hippocrates, the father of modern medicine, recognized this connection more than two thousand years ago. He noted: "Some patients, though conscious that their condition is perilous, recover their health simply through their contentment with the goodness of the physician." I believe this observation helps explain why the religious faith of a physician can be so important to many Christian patients. It connects two powerful healing beliefs: the patient's faith in the physician *and* the physician's faith in God as the

Great Physician. Faith in the God who heals truly is a faith that heals!

So what explains the cure of the woman with a chronic blood flow, a miracle described in Mark 5? Some readers see in her story the basis of "faith healing," so they seek out "faith healers" to cure their illnesses. Other people have a different understanding. They point to the woman's hopeful expectation—"If I just touch his clothes, I will be healed" (v. 28)—and understand what happened to her as an example of how faith activated her own body's natural healing systems.

Whatever the truth in this instance, what remains certain is that our beliefs about reality—as much as or even more than reality itself—generate our physical reactions. So simply believing in the goodness of God may have health benefits. And if your faith in God does not instantly cure you physically, it can still lead to many other kinds of healing. There are no negative side effects to hope.

TAKE TIME TO PONDER

1. In what ways could your beliefs about your current situation be either benefiting or injuring your health?
2. When faced with a difficult situation, do you tend to believe the worst, or do you approach problems with a belief in the power of God to make all things work for good? Give a specific example from your own life.

TAKE TIME TO PRAY

Father, help me see Your goodness more clearly each day so that I can trust You more completely. I pray that, as I see and experience more of Your goodness, You will transform me so that I will better reflect to others Your goodness, Your love, and Your willingness to forgive. In Jesus' name, amen.

INSIGHT 45

THINK OF GOD,
NOT THE GRUDGE

~ ✦ ~

On my bed I remember you;
I think of you through the watches of the night.

Psalm 63:6

Many of us struggle more than necessary to forgive people who have hurt or disappointed us simply because we can't stop thinking about the harm they inflicted on us. We assume that, because the thought entered our head, we must think about it for as long as it remains there. We come to believe that we have no control over our thoughts, that we must think about and even dwell on whatever pops into our head. What choice do we have? A thought drifted into our head, so what else could we think about?

Actually, we have plenty of choices. God has given you and me the power to choose what we think about. We are not at the mercy of renegade thoughts. We do not have to think about the same upsetting things over and over again. We do not have to dwell on any old idea that pops into our head.

The Bible insists, in fact, that not only can we change our thoughts to more closely reflect God's beauty and holiness, but we *must* change them. "Brothers," Paul commanded on God's behalf, "stop thinking like children. In regard to evil be infants, but in your thinking be adults" (1 Corinthians 14:20). To the young believers at Ephesus, Paul wrote, "So I tell you this, and insist on it in the Lord, that you must no longer live as the Gentiles do, in the futility of their thinking" (Ephesians 4:17). And the apostle Peter told another group of believers, "Dear friends, this is now my second letter to you. I have written both of them as reminders to stimulate you to wholesome thinking" (2 Peter 3:1).

What do all these instructions have in common? Each one directs believers in Christ to *change their thinking* when their thoughts move in negative rather than positive directions.

In other words, you can—and must—take control of your thoughts. When you start thinking about that no-good, rotten scoundrel who treated you so unfairly and you begin to feel angry and anxious, put a stop to those unproductive thoughts by choosing to think about something else. Make the hard work of forgiveness easier by learning how to direct your thought life.

Although this process of taking charge of our thoughts takes practice, you can master it. I compare it to changing the channel on your television set. If you turn on your TV and a program you don't like fills the screen, what do you do? You change the channel. You don't sit there for an hour watching what you don't like (unless, of course, your spouse controls the remote), waiting for the next show to come along. That would be foolish! No, you change the channel to something you prefer.

You can do something very similar in your head. When upsetting thoughts pop into your mind, don't try to stop thinking about them. Instead, choose to think about something else. Picture what you're going to have for dinner, start planning your next vacation, try to recall details of the happiest day of your life, or imagine what it would be like to spend a day with your favorite hero. Or, even better, like King David, choose to meditate on the glories of your God: "On my bed I remember you; I think of you through the watches of the night" (Psalm 63:6).

So you don't like your current thoughts? Then change the channel. Think of God, not the grudge. You might not be able to stop stray thoughts from entering the airspace of your mind, but you certainly don't have to let them land.

TAKE TIME TO PONDER

1. What do you tend to do when unwanted thoughts pop into your head? Why?
2. Why would having better control of your thought life make the process of forgiveness easier?

TAKE TIME TO PRAY

Father, I know that a key to my growth in Christ—and my ability to forgive—is the discipline of learning to control my thought life. You have commanded me to choose my thoughts, so I know that—with Your help—it's possible. So, when ugly thoughts pop into my mind, remind me to change the channel—for Your glory and my benefit. In Jesus' name, amen.

INSIGHT 46

CHANGE THE CHANNEL

Finally, brothers, whatever is true, whatever is noble, whatever is right, whatever is pure, whatever is lovely, whatever is admirable—if anything is excellent or praiseworthy—think about such things.

Philippians 4:8

Since the advent of cable television, consumers have enjoyed a growing number of programming choices. It used to be that if your television set could receive a handful of VHF stations and one or two UHF stations, you were doing great. But these days, viewers in most locales can pick from literally hundreds of programs any moment of any day. They enjoy a smorgasbord of channel choices, from sports to science, history to health, music to movies, real estate to religion, golf to gardening, and just about anything in between.

Do you realize that, wherever you live and whatever time of day, you have an even broader selection of "thought channels" from which to choose? So, if your default channel keeps replaying the same old story of how someone treated you unfairly, you can immediately switch to any one of an almost limitless number of better mental channels.

"Sounds great," you say, "but I don't have much of an imagination."

Whether or not that's the case (and I doubt that it is), let me suggest that you let the apostle Paul's words in Philippians 4:8 serve as a jumping-off point for tuning in to some new and healthier mental channels.

Whatever is true: Don't listen to the hurtful lies communicated in a distorted picture of your personal history. Focus on what is true. Don't settle for conjecture or assumption. What do you *know* is true about what happened? What would all reports, from all points of view, consider to be the truth?

Whatever is noble: What would you consider "noble" in the world around you? Whom do you most admire? What charities do you most respect? What admirable goals do you desire to achieve in your life?

Whatever is right: There's a lot wrong with this world, but what do you see that's right? What specific causes do you champion? Who are your heroes? What choices can you make today that will make your life—and even help make this world—a better place?

Whatever is pure: Why does the Bible call Jesus "a lamb without blemish or defect" (1 Peter 1:19)? Think about your Savior's purity. Why do we call babies "innocent"? Why does God demand moral purity from His children?

Whatever is lovely: What do you think makes a painting or sculpture beautiful? Who is the loveliest person you know—and what is lovely about him or her? With what words and images would you describe heaven for someone who has never heard of it?

Whatever is admirable: In the world of politics, whom do you most admire? Which religious leader? What historical figures earn your applause? What community initiatives do you admire?

Whatever is excellent: When you think of "excellence," what comes to mind? Whom do you know—or know of—who strives for excellence? What would an excellent day look like for you?

Whatever is praiseworthy: What earns your praise? Who praised you as a child? What kind of praise most encourages you today? What aspects of your life are worthy of God's praise right now?

These questions are merely suggestions intended to get you started. Once you've practiced changing mental channels, you'll find thousands of healthy thoughts that can build you up rather than tear you down.

TAKE TIME TO PONDER

1. What is your mental "default channel"? Give just a brief description. Don't dwell on it!
2. What steps can you take to best practice the command in Philippians 4:8 to dwell on the better things in life? Which step will you take this week?

TAKE TIME TO PRAY

Father, a whole universe of thought choices exists. Please help me not get stuck on a few unhelpful channels. Open my eyes to all the positive options and train me to focus on the thoughts that build me up rather than tear me down. In Jesus' name, amen.

INSIGHT 47

THE HEALTH BENEFITS OF LOVE

It is not good for the man to be alone.
Genesis 2:18

Recent research indicates that love is critically important to your health.

In one fascinating laboratory study, researchers accidentally discovered the protective health benefits of love. They fed a group of rabbits a high-cholesterol diet to study the impact of nutrition on heart disease, yet only half the rabbits developed the expected coronary ailment. Somehow, the other half seemed to remain quite healthy despite their unhealthy diet.

The outcome both baffled and intrigued the scientists. What could have possibly protected those rabbits from heart disease? The scientists knew it couldn't be genetic, for they were using laboratory rabbits specifically bred to have the same genetic makeup. When the scientists carefully retraced every step of their experiment, searching for that one differentiating variable, they discovered that the nighttime laboratory technician was an animal lover. While feeding the rabbits, she picked each one of them up and cuddled them. Not being very tall, however, she could not reach the rabbits in the top row of cages. Incredibly, the rabbits in the bottom row of cages escaped most of the harmful effects of the high-cholesterol diet while all of those in the upper row contracted heart ailments. The difference in health outcomes for those rabbits in the lower cages was the result of love.

Studies of humans also indicate that social support protects us against many diseases. In Alameda County, California, for instance, a study of 6,848 residents showed that those with many close social ties had a lower risk of death compared to people with few social ties. Even people with unhealthy lifestyles but close connections with others lived longer than people with healthy behaviors who lacked close social ties. Note the study's key finding: *social isolation is a risk factor for illness.*

In a number of studies, regular involvement in a church also appears to be associated with better health, probably due in large measure to religion's promotion of social support and the sense of belonging it can offer.

Another study of 91,909 individuals living in Washington County, Maryland, found that fewer deaths occurred among people who attended church at least once a week than among those who attended church less frequently. The church-going group suffered 50 percent fewer deaths from coronary disease; 56 percent fewer from emphysema; 74 percent fewer from cirrhosis; and 53 percent fewer deaths due to suicide. Yet another study, conducted in the Carolinas, found—after socioeconomic status and health behavior were factored out—a statistically significant lower mortality rate among church members compared to people who had no church affiliation. Going to church regularly can literally save your life!

In addition to social support, churches encourage people to care for one another. Volunteer activities and helping others enhance our well-being. This is especially true for older adults, many of whom are feeling less valued by society. Helping others gives one a sense of usefulness and purpose. Some researchers also believe that altruism may even help slow down the inevitable deterioration of the immune system as a person ages. Tests conducted at the Menninger Clinic seem to confirm the beneficial effect of love on the immune system. People involved in loving action produced white blood cells that were significantly more active in fighting infection. As a result, these people suffered fewer colds and had higher levels of endorphins (brain chemicals that positively affect moods). Choosing to set aside our own concerns and reaching out to others also lowers stress and therefore minimizes the negative health consequences associated with elevated stress levels.

As each of us knows in our heart and as science supports, we all need to love and be loved. Our involvement in both giving love and receiving it adds richness and texture to life like nothing else can.

TAKE TIME TO PONDER

1. How socially connected are you? Identify close friends, important relationships, and supportive social networks. If the list is short, what will you do to expand it? Be specific.
2. Would your social connections improve or increase if you more regularly practiced forgiveness? Explain your answer.

TAKE TIME TO PRAY

Father, it should not surprise me that, as the God who is love, You have created men and women who need to both give and receive love in order to thrive. Help me get better both at giving love and receiving love, and show me those relationships where forgiveness would help love thrive. In Jesus' name, amen.

INSIGHT 48

GOD'S PRESCRIPTION FOR HEALTH

᠁

Is any one of you sick? He should call the elders of the church to pray over him and anoint him with oil in the name of the Lord. And the prayer offered in faith will make the sick person well; the Lord will raise him up. If he has sinned, he will be forgiven.

James 5:14–15

Surveys indicate that 76 percent of Americans consider prayer an important part of their daily life. The fact that prayer has been used as a source of healing throughout the millennia and across all cultures suggests that it does indeed provide great value. So we pray.

But can science prove that prayer actually works? Apparently so, for in more than 130 controlled laboratory studies, prayer appeared to bring about measurable health benefits. Not a single study proved prayer to be harmful.

Science, however, cannot tell us how prayer works or exactly when it might work, but science does appear to confirm the efficacy of prayer. Some would argue that prayer works only because of the psychological benefits of positive thinking. After all, people who pray express their hope for and even expectation of a positive outcome.

Well-accepted, double-blind studies, however, suggest that something more than positive thinking is going on in prayer. Dr. Randolph C. Byrd of San Francisco General Hospital conducted a groundbreaking study on prayer in 1988. His double-blind study of 393 random coronary-care patients took place over a period of ten months. Members of one hospitalized group received intercessory prayer from Christians they never met while members of the control group had no one assigned to pray for them. These control patients more frequently required ventilatory assistance, antibiotics, and diuretics than patients in the group who were prayed for. This study clearly suggests that intercessory prayer for patients has beneficial therapeutic effects on them.

These findings may help explain why the practice of prayer is consistently ranked as the top coping method for dealing with trauma, especially for the elderly. In fact, among people age sixty-five and older, prayer is the most frequent coping strategy for dealing with loss, conflict, and stress.

A nationwide poll asking doctors whether they believe patients benefit from prayer and whether they themselves pray for patients also supported the positive role prayer plays in healing. Half of the doctors questioned said that they believe prayer helps patients; two-thirds of them reported praying for a patient.

So that's the current take of science on the effectiveness of prayer. As far as the Bible is concerned, of course, prayer and healing go hand in hand. James instructed sick believers to call for the elders of the church to pray for them and anoint them with oil, and he probably had in mind a medicinal use of oil rather than a sacramental one. For one thing, the word translated "anoint" is not the normal term used to describe anointing rites. History also makes it clear that, in New Testament times, oil was very often used as medicine. Many biblical scholars conclude that James is prescribing both prayer and medicine.

And we should not overlook that James's counsel includes forgiveness. Prayer and medicine can bring healing, but so can forgiveness. That's why James said that the application of prayer and oil, mixed with faith and forgiveness, will bring beneficial results.

How many believers get physically sick each year because they obsess on the faults of other people rather than extending to them forgiveness? More people than we'll ever know, I would guess. After all, God says health comes with prayer, faith, medicine, and forgiveness. We would be unwise to ignore any element of His divine prescription.

Take Time to Ponder

1. When has God used prayer to bring healing to you or to someone close to you? Be specific.
2. Why do you think God speaks about prayer, medicine, faith, forgiveness, and healing all together?

Take Time to Pray

Father, thank You for the marvelous gift of prayer. It still amazes me that You love us so much that You have given us a way to communicate with You so intimately and so constantly—not only to request Your healing touch but also to bask in Your presence. And as I walk in Your forgiving presence, Lord, transform me into a forgiving person. In Jesus' name, amen.

INSIGHT 49

A TREMENDOUS SOURCE
OF STRENGTH AND HEALTH

⁂

Let us not give up meeting together, as some are in the habit of doing,
but let us encourage one another.

Hebrews 10:25

Do you know of people who stay away from church because they hold a grudge against someone in that church? "I'm not ever going to cross the threshold of that place until *that woman* apologizes to me," such individuals may say. "I won't give her the satisfaction of thinking she's gotten away with hurting me!"

So in an effort to punish the one who hurt them, they stay home rather than go to church—and by doing so, they hurt themselves far more than the person they intended to penalize.

We can hold a grudge against someone in church just as easily as we can nurture a grudge against anyone else, and when we do, we suffer the same physical and emotional consequences characteristic of a refusal to forgive someone in any other sphere of life. But if we allow that grudge to keep us away from what Paul called "the body of Christ," the church, the damage we do to ourselves is even greater.

145

Consider a two-year study of elderly individuals forced to move from their homes. It revealed that people who were more religiously committed had a lower mortality rate than people who were less religious. The comfort the religious people derived from their faith proved to be the key to their survival.

The same is true for people dealing with medical issues ranging from heart disease to cancer. Studies indicate a health benefit for those who regularly draw strength from their church. For instance, cancer patients who scored high on spiritual well-being experienced less anxiety than those with a lower score—and relief from anxiety and pain are important in the successful treatment of cancer.

Also, in a systematic review of the literature on the relationship between religious commitment and hypertension, researchers found that religious commitment (measured by frequency of church attendance) was associated with lower blood pressure 90 percent of the time. These findings led to the conclusion that religion appears to help reduce hypertension. Studies like this contributed to an important conclusion in the 1987 report by the U.S. Department of Health and Human Services: for the first time, the government advocated that the church and the medical community work together to detect, treat, and prevent health problems.

The bottom line is that regular involvement at church—that being actively engaged with other committed believers in service and worship—improves your physical health, your emotional outlook, and your walk with God. So if you are allowing a lack of forgiveness to keep you away from church and are therefore uninvolved with other believers, then you're not only permitting your unresolved anger to cause you untold physical difficulties, but you're also cutting yourself off from a tremendous source of strength and health.

God knew what is best for us when He issued this command through the writer of Hebrews: "Let us not give up meeting together, as some are in the habit of doing, but let us encourage one another" (10:25). Even in New Testament days, some people had given up the habit of gathering together as a church—and God said, in effect, "Don't do that! You need the encouragement and support that My church provides. I didn't create you to live alone. You need others in your life who also know and love Me. Being part of that community is crucial to your physical, emotional, and spiritual well-being."

When conflicts and disputes arise between you and other people (especially other believers)—and they will—I encourage you to practice forgiving one another. Doing so will be good for you.

TAKE TIME TO PONDER

1. In what ways are you regularly involved at church?
2. Does a lack of forgiveness ever keep you away from church? If so, what are you missing out on?

TAKE TIME TO PRAY

Father, the church is one of Your best gifts to Your people, but please help me appreciate it even more. Remind me to be quick to forgive when someone—especially someone in the church—wrongs me, and help me be a reason why others enjoy coming to church, rather than a reason why they might stay home. In Jesus' name, amen.

Insight 50

An Unbreakable Link

*But one thing I do: forgetting what lies behind and reaching forward
to what lies ahead, I press on toward the goal.*

Philippians 3:13–14 NASB

Desmond Tutu, Anglican Archbishop emeritus of Cape Town, South Africa, once declared, "There can be no future without forgiveness."

He was absolutely right.

Tutu knew that only through forgiveness could the deeply divided peoples of South Africa create a future of hope for their violence-torn nation. He knew that creating a healthy community requires generous and ongoing expressions of forgiveness, for imperfect people—and that's all of us—can live together in peace only when we forgive each other for the terrible ways we sometimes hurt one another.

Our commitment to forgive can also energize our desire to move from what *was* toward what *can be*. In fact, an unbreakable link connects forgiveness and hope. How is it possible to let go of a yesterday filled with hurt and escape a present sense of bitterness in order to build a tomorrow characterized by hope and healing? I know of no path except forgiveness. Without forgiveness, we will continue to be emotionally stuck in an ugly past with its anger, hatred, and recrimination. With forgiveness, however, we can take bold and strong steps toward a bright future. All of us. Together.

And think about it. Wouldn't you prefer to work toward the kind of future you really want rather than grouse about a past you can't change? You may think you need to balance the scales of justice and make life fair once again, but my guess is that—in your heart of hearts—what you really want is to enjoy life, to laugh again and smile. When you forgive, you exchange the hopelessness of your past for a future filled with hope. And isn't that one of the best trades of all time?

When you forgive, you set yourself free to pursue a life bursting with fresh possibilities. But when you focus on the horrible people who have hurt you, you sabotage your future. It's as if you say, every day of your life, "It's bad now—and it's going to be worse tomorrow." So you sacrifice a sunny future on the altar of a dark and miserable past.

The apostle Paul refused to do that. Even while he was in chains in a dank Roman prison for doing nothing more than spreading the word about the resurrected Christ, he refused to blame his captors, indulge in fantasies of revenge, or moan about his unfair treatment. Instead, he told some Christian friends, "One thing I do: forgetting what lies behind and reaching forward to what lies ahead, I press on toward the goal" (Philippians 3:13–14 NASB). In other words, Paul left the past behind in order to build the future. He rejected vengeance and embraced hope.

Paul had instructed others to be "imitators of God" by practicing forgiveness (Ephesians 4:32–5:1), and he practiced what he preached. And what drove him to this practice? What motivated the apostle's behavior? Paul had a vision of a glorious future where the hurts of his past had no power over him: "I want to know Christ and the power of his resurrection and the fellowship of sharing in his sufferings, becoming like him in his death, and so, somehow, to attain to the resurrection from the dead" (Philippians 3:10–11).

Forgiveness is a force so powerful that it has the ability to shape the future—*your* future. When you embrace forgiveness, you forge an unbreakable link with hope. And who wouldn't choose to live with a bright optimism about the future rather than a dark pessimism about the past?

Take Time to Ponder

1. When have you either experienced or seen the link between forgiveness and hope? Be specific.
2. What kind of a bright future could forgiveness help make possible in your own life?

Take Time to Pray

Father, I believe that Desmond Tutu was right when he said, "There is no future without forgiveness." Like every other human being on the planet, I need hope for the future in order to keep moving ahead, but I also want to help nurture hope in the hearts of others. So help me to both become a forgiving person and, by my example, help others find hope. In Jesus' name, amen.

INSIGHT 51

DON'T TRY IT YOURSELF

"How many loaves do you have?" Jesus asked.
"Seven," they replied, "and a few small fish."

Matthew 15:34

A friend of mine shattered his left elbow about a year ago. Despite his wife's sensible request that he wait until he could get some help to scrape a little paint off a window high above their front door, he quietly got out a ladder, leaned it against the interior wall, climbed twelve feet or so into the air, fiddled with a razor-blade device to try to remove the paint—and then watched, dumbfounded, as the ladder slid out from under him and down the wall, crashed onto the hardwood floor, and shot toward the opposite wall, smashing a large hole in it. Moments later, my friend was on his way to the emergency room, offering another argument against the saying "If you want something done right, you have to do it yourself."

Of course you and I should do many things on our own. But a great many other things cannot and should never be attempted on our own. We need help, and to try to do certain jobs without assistance leads to things like unexpected visits to hospitals.

Yet we human beings like to try doing things on our own, don't we? This "I'll do it myself" tendency affects many aspects of life, perhaps including how we deal with people who hurt us. Far too often when someone hurts us, we seek justice by trying on our own to make things fair. We may, for instance, seek to hurt the one who wounded us. But such an effort doesn't ever really make life fair, does it? In fact, it almost always seems to make situations worse. We want to remove the paint that someone else left on our window, but by taking matters into our own hands, we wind up at the hospital, in worse pain than we were in when we began.

That's one reason why we have to learn that, when God calls us to forgive, He doesn't leave us on our own to complete the task. He's right there with us, holding the ladder and giving us the coaching and the resources we need in order to accomplish what He calls us to do.

Remember how Jesus fed the four thousand? Multitudes had gone to a remote spot to hear Him speak and see Him heal the sick. When He told His disciples that He didn't want to send the crowd away without giving them something to eat, His men looked at each other and said, "Where could we get enough bread in this remote place to feed such a crowd?" (Matthew 15:33). It was impossible, of course—if they tried to do it on their own. The Twelve simply didn't have the resources.

And this is where the story gets really interesting. Jesus did not say, "OK, boys, stand back. You can't do this, but I can—and without your help." Instead, He asked His disciples what resources they did have. The grand total came to seven loaves of bread and a few small fish. You know the rest of the story: Jesus took these very limited resources, multiplied them, and asked His disciples to distribute the food. In this way, four thousand men plus an unspecified number of women and children were fed.

And what does this miracle story have to do with forgiveness? Well, Jesus doesn't want you to try to balance the scales by getting back at the people who hurt you. Neither does He expect you to forgive them on your own power, nor does He let you sit back and watch Him do all the work. When you trust God, He takes your meager resources and multiplies them in order to achieve something that delights His heart: a person who forgives as He does. You will never know all the blessings that God is capable of providing until you take a step of faith in Him.

By the way, a week or so after my friend had surgery to repair his elbow, a buddy from his church offered to go to his house and take care of the window. He used the same ladder and the same razor-blade device my friend had used. This time, however, someone held the ladder. The whole operation took about thirty seconds, and no one wound up in the emergency room.

TAKE TIME TO PONDER

1. What would you like to do the next time someone hurts you? How can you let your awareness of how much you have been forgiven influence your forgiveness of someone else? Explain.

2. Why do we human beings need Jesus' help in forgiving people who have hurt us? What specific help to forgive do you need today?

TAKE TIME TO PRAY

Father, I need You to take my limited resources—my limited abilities to forgive and to love my enemy—and multiply them just as Your Son, Jesus, did when He fed the crowd of more than four thousand. I cannot make certain relationships right on my own, and I know You will not do my work of forgiveness for me. So please take what limited abilities I have to love and forgive and enlarge them so that I can extend the grace of forgiveness to others even as You have extended that grace to me. In Jesus' name, amen.

INSIGHT 52

A LIFE WITHOUT POISON

⁂

Create in me a pure heart, O God,
and renew a steadfast spirit within me.

Psalm 51:10

I used to be the director of a Christian summer camp. Every week 125 city kids came out to the country to learn about the Creator and His creation. One year, when my nature counselor was driving through the western desert to join us, he captured a rattlesnake to add some excitement to the displays in the nature building.

I wasn't exactly thrilled with the idea of having a rattlesnake among all those children. But my nature director assured me he would keep the snake locked securely in a cage. Our fanged guest did indeed excite the kids, so against my better judgment, the rattlesnake stayed.

Everything went well during the first three weeks of camp. Then it happened! The rattlesnake escaped from its cage and hid somewhere in the nature building. Without telling the campers why, I immediately sealed off the building and made it strictly off-limits to all of them. I told the kids, "There's no better place to study nature than out in nature itself."

Once the nature building was empty of campers, we

carefully searched every nook and cranny, cautiously moving each item the rattlesnake might be hiding under or behind. I feared that even with such vigilance, someone might get bitten, so I called the hospital to ask that they have some antivenom ready just in case.

Fortunately, we found the snake all curled up and not in the mood to strike. We quickly captured it, returned it to its cage, and sent it away from the campgrounds, never to return.

Rattlesnake venom definitely has a way of killing people, but it's not the only kind of poison that can kill. Anger can do the same thing. And whether you're dealing with venom from a viper or resentment from a run-in, if you don't do something—and quickly—about the poison coursing through your veins, you can expect that, in a very short while, you will start experiencing some very, very unpleasant consequences.

You see, the human body is no more able to effectively rid itself of rattlesnake venom than it can effectively rid itself of resentment. In order to prevent either of these poisons from killing you once they've entered your body, you have to take deliberate action to counteract their natural and deadly tendencies.

Fortunately, cures for both toxins are available, but their effectiveness depends on how quickly you act. Antivenom treatments can save the life of someone bitten by a rattler, and forgiveness can save the life of someone poisoned by resentment. The truly amazing thing is that, with the latter, God has provided such a way to completely restore a soul eaten away by bitterness and long-time grievance, that it's almost like getting a brand-new life.

I believe the psalmist had something very much like that in mind when he prayed, "Create in me a pure heart, O God, and renew a steadfast spirit within me."

Imagine what it would be like to have all the poison

removed from your soul. No more bitterness. No more obsession with revenge. No more waking up in the middle of the night with the same angry tape playing in your mind. No more feelings of frustrated rage, helplessness, or weary resignation to a bleak future.

Wouldn't that feel good?

Well, when you pray as did the psalmist—"Create in me a pure heart, O God"—that is what you're requesting. You aren't merely asking God to remove all the disagreeable feelings that clutter and foul your heart. You ask for a new heart, a pure heart, a heart that looks a good deal like His own loving heart.

In other words, a heart capable of forgiving.

TAKE TIME TO PONDER

1. What, if anything, is keeping you from letting go of the bitterness in your heart? What will you do about that barrier?

2. What do you think it would be like to have God give you a clean heart?

TAKE TIME TO PRAY

Father, I want and need the clean heart that only You can provide. I long to know the joys and delights of wanting what You want and pursuing what You pursue. So please help me develop a heart of forgiveness, Lord, and in that way gain the cleaner heart that I so desperately need. In Jesus' name, amen.

INSIGHT 53

A TASTE OF HEAVEN

~C~

He will wipe every tear from their eyes.
There will be no more death or mourning or crying or pain,
for the old order of things has passed away.

Revelation 21:4

The Bible talks a lot about tears, and most passages refer to their abundance in this broken world of ours.

"My eyes pour out tears to God," cried Job (Job 16:20).

"All night long I flood my bed with weeping and drench my couch with tears," wrote David (Psalm 6:6).

"My tears have been my food day and night," sighed a son of Korah (Psalm 42:3).

"You have fed them with the bread of tears; you have made them drink tears by the bowlful," lamented Asaph (Psalm 80:5).

"I saw the tears of the oppressed—and they have no comforter," declared Solomon (Ecclesiastes 4:1).

"I . . . say again even with tears, many live as enemies of the cross of Christ," grieved the apostle Paul (Philippians 3:18)

Even the shortest verse in the Bible reminds us that "Jesus wept" (John 11:35).

I don't know of anyone whose life has been void of tears, and I'm guessing you don't either. These unavoidable tears remind us that we live in a broken world where pain and suffering are inevitable. Perhaps it's because so many tears wet the pages of His Book that God begins His final description of heaven with the promise "He will wipe every tear from their eyes."

I never tire of reading those words. What a beautiful picture! Jesus will put this broken world back together again. Tears and sorrow will become a thing of the past. God will finally make life fair again, and His absolute and perfect justice shall reign over the new heaven and the new earth.

I look forward to living in that world without tears—or, more accurately, a world where tears have become unnecessary. But before then, even as we live on this fallen planet, I believe we can enjoy a taste of that world to come. Let me explain.

Remember when Jesus told His disciples that some of them would catch a glimpse of His kingdom long before it arrived? Just six days afterward He asked Peter, James, and John to accompany Him up to the top of a "high mountain," and there He "was transfigured before them. His face shone like the sun, and his clothes became as white as the light. Just then there appeared before them Moses and Elijah, talking with Jesus" (Matthew 17:1–3). What a joyous reunion—and unexpected too. In fact, the sudden appearance and then the quick departure of these Old Testament heroes so disoriented Peter that he made a foolish suggestion about building shelters for the heavenly visitors, a suggestion which Jesus graciously ignored. The Bible says that Peter "did not know what he was saying" (Luke 9:33). Nevertheless, the three dazed disciples got a taste of heaven long before they stepped foot on its streets of gold.

Do you know that you can also get a taste of heaven long before you arrive there? A taste comes whenever you choose to forgive.

Heaven is a very forgiving place. It has to be if it's to open its gates to let in spiritual delinquents like you and me! So whenever you forgive, a little bit of heaven breaks through the clouds and shines into your world, if only for a brief moment, making it "as white as the light."

Do you want a taste of heaven? You can if you really want to. All it takes is a little forgiveness on your part.

Take Time to Ponder

1. Why can the forgiveness that only Christ offers put your life back together again? Share some details about what that would look like for you.

2. What tears could you help wipe away if you chose to forgive someone right now?

Take Time to Pray

Father, I look forward to the day when You will wipe away every tear, including my own. I thank You and praise You for sending Your Son, Jesus, into this world to make my forgiveness—and my forgiveness of others—possible. And now, Lord, use me to give others a taste of heaven by enabling me to forgive them just as You have forgiven me. In Jesus' name, amen.

INSIGHT 54

NO SECOND THOUGHTS

But with you there is forgiveness;
therefore you are feared.

Psalm 130:4

Can you imagine if God's forgiveness looked like ours?

"I will forgive you *if* you do what I want you to do."

"I will forgive you, *but* you need to make some major changes first."

"I will forgive you *when* you get your act together."

"I will forgive you *only* if you demonstrate enough remorse for what you did to me."

Perhaps the psalmist had such a laundry list of conditions in mind when he wrote, "If you, O LORD, kept a record of sins, O Lord, who could stand? But with you there is forgiveness; therefore you are feared" (Psalm 130:3–4). The psalmist fears and honors God as he rejoices because he knows that the forgiveness that saves him flows completely and absolutely out of God's grace, mercy, and love. He does not earn a bit of it—and whenever we realize that our very life depends on the goodness of Another, reverential fear tends to fill our heart.

This reverent and right fear of God, however, is not the focus of this psalm. Instead, the spotlight is on the psalmist's sense of wonder and even astonishment at the complete and total forgiveness God offers to every man and woman who place their genuine trust in Him. The psalmist recognizes how far distant his sins *should* remove him from his holy and awesome God. No one has to convince this godly man that he is unworthy! But what he cannot get over, what he cannot begin to fathom, is the absolutely clean slate the Lord of the universe offers him when he chooses to surrender his life to Him.

When was the last time you meditated on God's complete forgiveness of your sins? When did you last thank Him for lavishing His free and unconditional grace upon you? Do you recall when you last thought about the full implications of the fact that Jesus "is able to save completely those who come to God through him, because he always lives to intercede for them" (Hebrews 7:25)?

Unlike many of us human beings, Jesus says to you, "I will forgive you." Period. That's it. That's all. He doesn't mention any ifs, ands, buts, whens, or onlys. The one thing Jesus asks you to do is accept His complete forgiveness by placing your faith in Him—and then let His grace transform your life. So, reverently ponder all that He has done for you, gratefully watch how He moves in your life, and know that you are "being transformed into his likeness with ever-increasing glory, which comes from the Lord, who is the Spirit" (2 Corinthians 3:18).

And all of this—every bit of it—is yours through the full, free, and absolute forgiveness that God offers you. He will never stop to consider whether you are worthy of being forgiven. He will never decide that you are simply too much trouble to keep forgiving. He will never grow weary of having to forgive you. He will never wish that He had added some conditions to His offer of forgiveness. You and I might do that, but our God never will. Once you place your faith in Jesus, you are completely and fully forgiven. Period.

TAKE TIME TO PONDER

1. Do you believe you are fully forgiven? Why or why not—and to whom will you talk to about any doubts you have?

2. Why is it important to believe that there is nothing you can do to forfeit God's full and complete forgiveness? What impact should this truth have on your ability to forgive others?

TAKE TIME TO PRAY

Father, I marvel at Your forgiveness—complete, total, and constant. Give me the grace to continue to be grateful for what You have done for me—and to extend forgiveness to others. Also, please grant me a heart that fears You as the psalmist did. You are amazing, Lord! In Jesus' name, amen.

Insight 55

An Eternal Difference

≈C≈

*Jesus said, "Father, forgive them, for they do not
know what they are doing."*

Luke 23:34

Was anyone ever treated more unfairly than Jesus?

He came into the world because of His pure love for lost
people; He left it because of some of those people's snarling
hatred.

He taught nothing but truth; at the trial that led to His
death, He heard nothing but lies.

He cared for each of His friends; they all deserted Him
when He needed them most.

He healed the sick and cured the lame; He Himself was
beaten, scourged, and crucified on a Roman cross.

He honored God with His life; the world blasphemed
God through His death.

Who would blame Jesus if, as He hung on the cross, He

had cursed His persecutors? Who would fault Jesus if He had asked His Father to rain down fire and brimstone on His murderers?

Yet Jesus did neither of these things. After the world had arrested Him, abused Him, condemned Him, whipped Him, mocked Him, and nailed Him to a cross, it could do nothing more to Him. But Jesus could still do—and He did—much for the world.

"Father," He cried out from the cross, "forgive them, for they don't know what they're doing."

Jesus made an infinite and eternal difference for you and me at Calvary. He did not stay in heaven and watch us destroy ourselves. Despite our hideous persecution of Him—and, make no mistake, your sins and mine put Jesus on the cross as much as the sins of the lying Jewish religious leaders and cruel Roman soldiers did—He forgave us.

"Greater love has no one than this," Jesus had declared earlier, "that he lay down his life for his friends" (John 15:13). Long before His arrest, His trial, and His execution, Jesus knew that He would be the one laying down His life for His friends. Many times He had tried to tell His disciples, "We are going up to Jerusalem, and everything that is written by the prophets about the Son of Man will be fulfilled. He will be handed over to the Gentiles. They will mock him, insult him, spit on him, flog him and kill him. On the third day he will rise again." Yet the meaning of His words was never clearly understood by those who heard them. According to the Gospel writer Luke, "The disciples did not understand any of this. Its meaning was hidden from them, and they did not know what he was talking about" (Luke 18:31–34).

Yet, Jesus still loved. He still forgave. In His ultimate act of self-sacrifice, Jesus demonstrated both His desire to love us and His willingness to forgive us.

How should we respond to His immeasurable love?

What should His great forgiveness prompt in us?

Well, I find it hard to think of a better response than committing yourself to a lifestyle of forgiveness. Of course, forgiveness cannot undo the damage already caused by evil. As someone wisely said—and you may have to read this sentence twice—"Forgiveness is giving up all hope for a better past." What's done is done, but your forgiveness most certainly can keep the damage from spreading any further.

TAKE TIME TO PONDER

1. Have you accepted Christ's forgiveness? If so, when and why? If not, why not?
2. Why can forgiving someone who has hurt you keep the damage of some past event from spreading any further? As you answer this question, refer to a specific incident from your own life.

TAKE TIME TO PRAY

Father, sometimes all I can do when I consider Jesus' ultimate sacrifice for me is to say, "Thank You." Your Word tells me that when I was still in rebellion against You, Jesus died for me. And that really is love! That is grace! And now that I have received Your love and grace, use me to pour Your love and grace into the lives of others. In Jesus' name, amen.

INSIGHT 56

WHY DID JESUS COME?

For God so loved the world that He gave His only begotten Son,
that whoever believes in Him should not perish
but have everlasting life.

John 3:16 NKJV

For good reason John 3:16 is perhaps the most quoted verse in all of Scripture.

It wasn't too many years ago when you could hardly go to a baseball game, an auto race, a soccer match, or even a rodeo without someone waving a sign with the words of John 3:16 emblazoned on it. Whenever these signs showed up and whenever telecasts captured them on camera, people were reminded of God's amazing offer of forgiveness, even though the word *forgiveness* doesn't appear in the verse.

John 3:16 answers the question, "Why did Jesus come to this earth in the first place?" He didn't come primarily to serve as a great example of living a moral life that pleases God, although He certainly provides us with our best model for living a godly life. Jesus didn't come mainly to teach us advanced theology, although His words express the eternal and heavenly truth of His Father. Jesus didn't come chiefly to help us feel good about ourselves, although those who knew Him best also felt more confident and alive than they ever had before.

Instead, the purpose of Christ's earthly life was to make forgiveness possible. He Himself stated it clearly: "The Christ will suffer and rise from the dead on the third day, and repentance and forgiveness of sins will be preached in his name to all nations" (Luke 24:46–47). ·

Long before Jesus arrived on this planet, God had hinted at His plan of salvation. In fact, immediately after Adam and Eve's disobedience made His plan necessary, God announced what He intended to do. In what is sometimes called the *protoevangelion*, or first mention of the gospel, God promised that a descendant of Eve would one day destroy Satan at great personal cost (Genesis 3:15). The writer of Hebrews explained how Jesus fulfilled that prophecy: "Since the children have flesh and blood, he [Jesus] too shared in their humanity so that by his death he might destroy him who holds the power of death—that is, the devil—and free those who all their lives were held in slavery by their fear of death" (Hebrews 2:14–15).

And, while Genesis contains the first biblical prophecy of how Jesus would make our forgiveness possible, the last book of the Bible tells us that God designed His plan of salvation even before He created the world. In Revelation 13:8, John describes Jesus as "the Lamb that was slain from the creation of the world." Do you see how the entire Bible is really a story about forgiveness?

In eternity past, God developed His plan of forgiveness. When Adam and Eve sinned, God spoke about that plan. At Calvary, Jesus put God's plan of forgiveness into action. And we will enjoy eternity in heaven with our Father because of His willingness and ability to forgive us.

And that truth brings up another question. Since forgiveness has such a central place in the Bible and is what gives meaning to the life of Christ, shouldn't forgiveness also have a central place in the life of a Christian? God commands us to "live a life of love, just as Christ loved us and gave himself up for us as a fragrant offering and sacrifice to God" (Ephesians 5:2). Key to living a life of love is living a life of forgiveness: as God has forgiven us, so we are to forgive others.

Consider what may be the most important mathematical formula in the universe:

$$\begin{array}{r} \mathbf{1\ Cross} \\ \underline{+\ \mathbf{3\ Nails}} \\ =\ \mathbf{4\ given} \end{array}$$

Spend some time right now contemplating the price Jesus paid for the forgiveness of your sins. I can assure you that accepting His sacrifice on your behalf will change your life now and for eternity.

TAKE TIME TO PONDER

1. God knew that Adam and Eve's sin would cost Him the life of His Son, yet He went ahead and created us anyway. What does that truth say about God's love for us?

2. Why can the argument be made that there is nothing more important to living the Christian life—to living out the grace and love exemplified by Christ on the cross—than our ability to forgive?

TAKE TIME TO PRAY

Father, when I consider that, because of Your love, You provided for my forgiveness even before the creation of the world, I am filled with awe and gratitude. Now I pray that You would make me into a worthy ambassador of heaven by enabling me to imitate Your holy character, especially in the area of forgiveness. I love You, Lord! In Jesus' name, amen.

ABOUT THE AUTHOR

 D r. Dick Tibbits has worked in the field of behavioral care and spiritual health for more that thirty years. He has used his training and experience in counseling to help tens of thousands of people achieve a better life. Dr. Tibbits has dedicated his life to whole person health and designing life strategies that work in both the corporate world and private life.

Dr. Tibbits has a doctoral degree in psychology and is a licensed professional mental health counselor. He is also an ordained minister with a master's degree in theology. He has served as an adjunct professor for doctoral students at both Fuller Theological Seminary and Andrews University Theological Seminary. Dr. Tibbits is a certified supervisor with the Association for Clinical Pastoral Education. In addition, Dr. Tibbits trained at the Harvard University Mind-Body-Spirit Institute and worked collaboratively with professionals from Stanford University and Florida Hospital on his pioneering clinical research.

Dr. Tibbits has spoken on the healing power of forgiveness to professional and private audiences around the world, including Australia, New Zealand, Hong Kong, the Philippines, India, and Switzerland. He has presented his research at Harvard, Mayo, Stanford, and Loma Linda as well as to conferences as diverse as The International Conference on Stress and The National Woman's Health Conference.

Dr. Tibbits currently serves as Chief People Officer at Florida Hospital, the largest admitting hospital in America. To find out more about Dr. Tibbits's work, visit him online at:

www.DickTibbits.com

For nearly one hundred years, the mission of Florida Hospital has been to help patients, guests, and friends achieve whole-person health and healing. With seven hospital campuses and sixteen walk-in medical centers, Florida Hospital cares for nearly one million patients every year. When Dr. Lydia Parmele, the first female physician in the state of Florida, and her medical team opened Florida Hospital in 1908, their goal was to create a healing environment where they not only treated illness but also provided the support and education necessary to help patients achieve mental, physical, spiritual, and social health—or, simply put, whole-person health.

In the 1990's Florida Hospital began working with the Disney Corporation to create a groundbreaking facility that would showcase the model of health care for the twenty-first century and stay on the cutting edge of medical technology as it develops. A team of medical experts, industry leaders, and health-care futurists designed and built a whole-person health hospital named Florida Hospital Celebration Health located in Disney's town of Celebration, Florida. Since opening its doors in 1997, Celebration Health has been awarded the Premier Patient Services Innovator Award as "The Model for Health-Care Delivery in the 21st Century." Over 17,000 surgeons have come to this state-of-the-art facility for surgical training. Additionally, the hospital has provided over 500 paid consultations and conducted 3,000 tours to leaders within the healthcare industry interested in studying the whole-person health business model.

Florida Hospital is committed to creating the ideal blend which transforms the typical hospital experience to one that has the warmth of a home and the cachet of a resort, all delivered within the context of the highest standard of patient safety. Our vision of health and healing embraces the whole person throughout his or her entire life. Our philosophy on health, places a premium on the value of every human being, the potential of the human spirit and the affirmation of the human body as the expression of God's creative energy. We therefore embrace everyone as a child of God, respect and dignity of individuality and value the richness of human diversity.

Today, Florida Hospital:

- Is ranked by the American Hospital Association as number one in the nation for inpatient admissions
- Is the largest provider of Medicare services in the country
- Performs the most heart procedures each year, making the number one hospital the leader in fighting America's number one killer—heart disease
- Operates many nationally recognized centers of excellence including Cardiology, Cancer, Orthopedics, Neurology & Neurosurgery, Digestive Disorder, and Minimally Invasive Surgery
- Is, according to *Fit Pregnancy* magazine, one of the "Top 10 Best Places in the Country to Have a Baby"

For more information about Florida Hospital and whole-person health products including books, music, videos, conferences, seminars, and other resources, please contact:

Florida Hospital Publishing
683 Winyah Drive, Orlando, FL 32803
Phone: 407-303-7711 • Fax: 407-303-1818
Email: healthproducts@flhosp.org
www.FloridaHospital.com • www.CreationHealth.com

Forgive to Live

HOW FORGIVENESS CAN SAVE YOUR LIFE.

We either become overwhelmed by life's difficulties or we become strengthened by life's hardest lessons. The difference is found in one's ability to forgive. Dr. Dick Tibbits shows you how forgiveness can effectively reduce your anger, drastically improve your health and put you in charge of your life again, no matter how deep your hurt.

AS YOU:

- come to a new understanding of what has happened to you.
  - discover what forgiveness does and doesn't mean.
  - take steps to reframe your grievance story.
  - stop giving control to the people and pains of the past.
  - get your life – and maybe even your health – back.
- find a freedom, peace...and strength you've never had.

The companion workbook to *Forgive to Live* that digs deeper and assists you in personally applying the material from Dr. Dick Tibbits.

WORKBOOK IS PERFECT FOR:

- Individuals as a companion to the main book

- Seminar participants

- Healthcare organizations and other corporations who want to train employees how to better handle stress, anger and hostility at the office to improve their working relationships

- Clinicians who want to teach patients specific interventions to lower hypertension and other stress-related health consequences

- Small study groups to help facilitate
- And discuss the sharing of ideas.

FLORIDA HOSPITAL
America's Trusted Leader
for Health & Healing

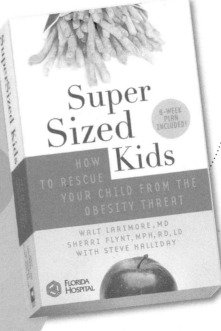